Moscow
Days

Moscow Days

*Life and Hard Times
in the New Russia*

Galina Dutkina

*Translated from the Russian
by Catherine A. Fitzpatrick*

KODANSHA INTERNATIONAL
New York • Tokyo • London

Kodansha America, Inc.
114 Fifth Avenue, New York, New York 10011, U.S.A.

Kodansha International Ltd.
17-14 Otowa 1-chome, Bunkyo-ku, Tokyo 112, Japan

Published in 1996 by Kodansha America, Inc.

Library of Congress Cataloging-in-Publication Data
Dutkina, G. (Galina), 1952–
  Moscow days : life and hard times in the New Russia / Galina
Dutkina ; translated from the Russian by Catherine A. Fitzpatrick.
    p.   cm.
  Includes index.
  ISBN 1–56836–066–5
    1. Moscow (Russia)—Social conditions. 2. Moscow (Russia)—
Economic conditions. 3. Post-communism—Russia (Federation)—
Moscow. 4. Russia (Federation)—Social conditions—1991–
5. Russia (Federation)—Economic conditions—1991–   6. Post-
communism—Russia (Federation)   I. Fitzpatrick, Catherine A.
II. Title.
HN530.2.M67D88   1995
306'.0947'312—dc20   95-37519

BOOK DESIGN BY LAURA HAMMOND HOUGH

Printed in the United States of America

96   97   98   99   00   RRD/H   10   9   8   7   6   5   4   3   2   1

To My Parents

And where do you fly to, Russia? Answer me! . . .
She doesn't answer. The carriage bells break into an
enchanted tinkling, the air is torn to shreds and turns
into wind, everything on earth flashes past, and, casting worried, sidelong glances, other nations and
countries step out of the way.

—Nikolai Gogol, *Dead Souls*

Contents

Preface

Russia's Not Laughing

Like people, years have their own faces. And like people, years have different dispositions. There are kind years and mean years, beautiful and ugly years, cheerful and sad years.

I lived through 1992 with the feeling that we were all sitting on a powder keg next to a camp fire—only a few sparks were needed for the explosive to ignite. Although there were a lot of sparks, trouble passed us by. The keg didn't blow up.

In 1993, starting in January, Russia began to bubble and boil like a kettle with a closed lid. What would pry it open—and when? The lid was blown off in September and October to the thunder of the White House shelling. The Russian porridge then boiled over and spilled into the December elections, when one quarter of the Russian voters chose Vladimir Zhirinovsky, an extreme nationalist who advocates a repartitioning of the world.

In 1994, we could not escape the sense of sheer astonishment, at times turning to shock. We never stopped being surprised—and surprising the whole world. Every month, every week, every day, came another amazing development. That's the kind of amazing country we have. And that's the kind of year we had.

A few years ago I visited Finland. Sitting in a snug little restaurant atop a revolving tower, I gazed at snug, sunfilled Helsinki and listened to the talk about everyday life there. I was having dinner with an extremely courteous, refined, middle-aged man, a retired teacher, and with utter sincerity he complained, "Finland is a wonderful country. Life here is wonderful, although it's a little bit expensive. But my pension is large, so I'm not griping. Yet . . . you know . . . it's so terribly boring here!"

"Well, why don't you annex yourselves to Russia?" I joked awkwardly. "Then you'll start having some fun." (To myself I thought, "Live through a few terrorist acts, a small ethnic conflict, and price hikes every week—and it won't seem so boring.")

My dinner partner froze in horror. My joke had fallen flat.

∾

There is a well-known tale about Timur Tamerlane, the famous fourteenth-century Mongol warlord who roundly defeated the Golden Horde. During one of his campaigns, Tamerlane imposed a harsh tribute on the inhabitants of a conquered city. His soldiers came to him and said, "People are refusing to pay the tribute, my lord. They claim that they don't have anything left."

"What are those people doing?"

"They're crying."

"Then off with you and take the tribute from them," ordered Tamerlane.

Then the warlord imposed a second tribute on the residents of the conquered city. Again, his soldiers came and said to him, "People are crying, oh lord. They say that you've taken everything away from them."

"If they're crying, that means it's not everything," replied Tamerlane. "Off with you and take tribute from them."

A third time the soldiers came to Tamerlane. "There isn't anything more for us to take, lord!"

"What are the people doing?" asked Tamerlane.

"They're laughing."

"Well, now, if they're laughing, that must mean that it really *is* everything."

What would Tamerlane say if he learned that the people had forgotten how to laugh?

People don't joke anymore in Russia. People no longer tell funny anecdotes about the leaders or about the popular fairy-tale character Ivan the Fool or the usual butt of ethnic humor, the Armenians or the Chukchi. Even the satirists and comedy writers have fallen silent.

Under Khrushchev, people laughed till their sides split. Under Brezhnev, people openly mocked things. Under Andropov and Chernenko, people made malicious fun of everything. Under Gorbachev, people amused themselves as best as they could. Even under Stalin, even under the threat of being shot, people still told jokes—they whispered them in your ear. But now there is only silence. No one is amused. No one is laughing. People are simply astonished.

A country that doesn't laugh is a sick country. People who have forgotten how to laugh are unwell; you can expect unpleasant surprises from them. Perhaps when you read this book you will understand how the Russian people got that way.

Moscow
Days

Chapter 1

The Good
and the Bad

When I was young I had a book of children's verse written by Vladimir Mayakovsky, the famous socialist poet. Many generations of Soviet children were raised on these rhymes. It was a rare child who did not know them by heart. The book began with a poem entitled "The Good and the Bad," and when I studied this little book I learned fundamental rules of life: Washing was good and being dirty was bad. Being a worker was good and being a member of the bourgeoisie was bad, since "hugely fat, like a butter blob/he loves to make others do his job." In these poems, white was white and black was black. The world seemed simple and precise, like a chessboard.

In those years I lived in a little provincial Russian city called Tambov. My father and mother had already made their way to Moscow, and I had been left with my grandmother. These were the last years of Khrushchev's rule and in the provinces, which he had brought to the brink of destruction, people were almost starving. Meanwhile, in Moscow, they'd almost achieved the ideal of Communism. When my mother visited me, she brought wonderful presents— little imported fur coats, fancy dresses and shoes, black and red caviar, fresh tomatoes and cucumbers, mandarin oranges (an inconceivable miracle in our frozen January!), rose-colored ham that melted in your mouth, and translucent, ripe cheese. The rolls, puffy and springy, that Mama stuffed by the dozens into her suitcase, instantly bounced up like rubber balls when they were freed from their prison because they were baked from good, white flour.

But in Tambov we had empty shelves, filth on the unwashed streets, and long, endless lines to the only little store in the district, waiting for "the fats," as people called them—that is, butter and margarine, which were sold only once a week. On teeth-chatteringly cold winter mornings, Grandmother woke me while it was still dark so we could get to the store in time to get a good place in line. Numbers marking our place were written on the palm of our hands with a chemical pencil. The numbers turned blue from sweat, but I wouldn't have washed them off for the world.

When I came to Moscow, I was overcome by the abundance of everything and even more startled by the contrast with the provinces. But soon Khrushchev was removed and Moscow's opulence also gradually disappeared until the shelves in the stores grew as empty and uninviting as those of my childhood.

By that time I had realized that not everything in the world was as simple and clear as it was in Mayakovsky's poems. In fact, the world was completely the opposite: white was black and black was white.

My ten-year-old daughter Dasha is growing up in a

different time, when children are no longer forced to learn Mayakovsky's poetry. Sometimes I get to thinking, does she see things as clearly as I did at one time? Can she tell the good from the bad? I don't think so because I can't always figure it out myself. The world has been turned upside down; it has lost the precision and clarity of a chessboard. The black has mingled with the white, and the white with the black, blending into a monotonous, depressing gray.

A Japanese television reporter who recently came to Moscow to collect material for a news show told me in amazement, "You Russians are constantly going on about how bad things are in your country, but the stores are filled with goods and people are buying lots of things. Explain to me exactly what it is that's bad here."

I couldn't answer this question intelligibly, not because I don't know the situation in Russia, but because it has now become very difficult to tell the good from the bad. Nevertheless, the question gave me pause, and I decided to try to look at Russia through the eyes of an outside observer. Our meeting had taken place in the newly remodeled Metropol Hotel, which glittered with marble, bronze, and crystal. Coming out of the glass doors to the street, I plunged back into Moscow's everyday life.

It was a lovely spring day. A fresh wind stirred the tree branches, still bare, and clouds glided across the blue sky like fuzzy little lambs. The red-bricked Kremlin towered triumphantly ahead, reminding me of the former greatness of Russia. Well-dressed little children holding hands and elegant ladies carrying bags filled with bright packages strolled down the clean sidewalks. Sleek foreign-made cars dashed along the road. Men in business suits and strapping fellows in leather jackets sat in the saloons.

The street was gaily decked with signs printed in the Roman alphabet, as if this were not the center of Moscow at all, but London or Paris. True, there was a sign in the Russian language nearby, but in smaller type and its message sent me back to another time when the signs were simple and true: Cheese. Sausage. Men's Clothing. Stationery. Now you can't figure out what is hidden behind the attractive names of the stores: Consi. Boutique. Nina Ricci. Nord American. R-Style. Rifle. Panasonic. Some are joint ventures and some belong to foreign capitalists. Everyone recognizes some of the names—even during the cold war we managed to read about "boutiques" and Nina Ricci—but many of the stores remain a mystery even to foreigners.

I picked a doorway at random and entered a store called Tamada. Tamada is a tiny foreign-style deli with a great variety of snacks that are very tasty and expensive, although not substantial enough for a real lunch or dinner. This store accepted dollars before January 1994, when it was prohibited by presidential decree to circulate foreign currency in Russia. (In December 1993 there were more than a thousand such "hard currency" stores in Moscow.) Now it accepts rubles, but if you want to badly enough, you can still pay in dollars. Next to a cash register there sits a girl with an iron box where dollars accepted from the customers are kept. In principle this is prohibited, but here, like everywhere else in Russia, a time-honored precept operates: If it's not allowed, but you really want to, then you can. I wonder if they pay their bribes to the inspectors in dollars or rubles?

I left through an underground passageway that led

onto the former Gorky Street, now restored to its original name, Tverskaya Street. A homeless man wearing hideous rags, most likely a fake beggar, was sitting by the exit. (He no doubt pays a handsome sum to the mafia or the police so as to be left alone in that choice location.)

Next I passed the gypsies, who had picked out a spot for themselves in front of the Intourist Hotel. They had trapped some unfortunate fellow and surrounded him, dancing and singing and begging money. It was a downright gypsy camp! If you give them your ring to tell your fortune upon, you will never see it again.

At the end of the passageway I came to a shop whose sign read Christian Dior. This seemed fairly obvious, but still, out of curiosity, I went inside. The display windows startle you with their depressing sameness and the prices are astronomical by Russian standards. Incidentally, the prices are written in dollars. The owners of expensive stores are too lazy to put new price tags out every day in keeping with the fluctuating exchange rate. They also don't want to scare away customers. The dollar price tags contain a very subtle psychological calculation: the ruble prices with their four zeroes stun the buyer, but for a person with money, $30 or $40 doesn't seem like such an incredible sum. I found mascara for $20, lipstick for $21. A poor selection. (For comparison, the average monthly wage in Russia is about $110).

The next store is a little shop called Donna. Then there's Queen of Saba. Until you enter one, you can't understand what these shops are selling. My eyes began to hurt from the signs and the advertisements.

No, I had no business being on Tverskaya Street. I decided to go to a big store, a department store. Right next to Red Square is such a store, called GUM, the Russian ac-

ronym for State Department Store. At least I would be able
to figure out everything there.

I walked in through the center doorway and was
literally blinded by the bright colors, mirrors, and lights. A
bouquet of multi-colored balloons floated below the ceiling.
There was a wonderful fragrance in the air. Rows of well-
dressed shoppers passed by. There was no pushing and shov-
ing and none of the lines that used to drive me crazy ten
years ago. Instead, ladies as graceful as does glided by with
men dressed to the nines. Poorly dressed people don't even
wander in here. This was the middle class and higher. Indeed, the horn of plenty!

I cheerfully pushed forward.

Instead of the open counters of the old days, now
there are little glassed-in shops, stores in themselves. The
signs in the display windows glow: Kodak. Sharp. Gabor.
Prince. Gillette.

One exotic spot is the German firm MCM—no shoppers here, but only silence and the scent of fine leather.
Within the store are fabulously expensive women's purses,
jeans, leather suitcases, and suits, all priced in deutsche
Marks. Another shop carries Italian chandeliers. The dish-
ware in the Tefal shop is quite elegant but completely beyond
the means of the Russian housewife. An iron was being sold
for $51, more than the monthly salary of a professor at Mos-
cow University.

The Polaroid counter didn't have a single browser,
even though ice-cream and balloon stands had been set up
outside the door. GUM used to have the best-tasting ice
cream in all of Moscow—vanilla, in crunchy waffle cones. I
remember playing hooky during my university days and
coming here to hang out. Now there's nothing like that ice

cream, only goods with foreign brandnames like Bounty, Snickers, Mars, Opal Fruit, and so on. The balloons are also foreign-made and crazy-looking. We didn't have balloons like that when I was a kid.

The items for sale on the first floor are almost all cosmetics and perfumes. Creams, eye shadows, perfumes, lotions, all kinds of nail polish, soaps, and gels. Yves Rocher, L'Oréal, Soap Berry Shops, Lakme, Fa . . . The scent was heavenly. At the counters were several interested young women, for whom beauty was more valuable than money.

Karstadt, Reebok, Adidas, Salamander. Shoes, men's clothing (usually just suit jackets and raincoats). Eyeglasses and Italian pizza. Coca-Cola. After about ten minutes my head began to ache. A particularly vivid impression remained from the housewares department, where brass bathroom fixtures cost $120 and curtain rods went for $230. Given the minimum monthly Russian salary of $9, and even the average salary of $110, the prices are unbelievable. But this is just the tip of the iceberg. I would advise genuine thrillseekers to go to a store called Zenith at the Sokolniki metro station, where an ordinary bathtub costs $2,000. Well, actually, it's not entirely ordinary—it's more of a triangular pool, and instead of faucets, it has chrome openings in the walls . . . but even the most ordinary bathtubs are not very cheap—at least $250 to $500. In short, whoever hasn't managed to get a new bathtub before all this price inflation is doomed to wash in his old one.

I decided to go up to the second floor, in hopes of finding a different scene up there. But no, it was all the same. Blinds. Jewelry. Men's jackets, suit coats, raincoats. There was a Russian-made woman's coat. Just looking at it gave me goose bumps. Then there was a Nina Ricci coat for

$1,330. That gave me goose bumps, too, but for a different reason. Then there were towels and sheets. Gloves, mittens, and hats. The ubiquitous "Russian theme" in the form of tasteless scarves with rose patterns, painted souvenir plates, and Gzhel porcelain. The Golden Dragon restaurant, the Cafe Copacabana. And to top it off, Furs of Russia.

A mink coat cost $2,600. A dark brown fox jacket sold for $2,300. A long coat made of some indeterminate animal's fur was almost $10,000. Perhaps this is cheap by American and European standards, but not for the Russian pocketbook. Nevertheless, there were some shoppers; a couple looked over the fox jacket. An emaciated girl with bowed legs and obviously unwashed hair was standing with a tough-looking fellow in a leather jacket, the uniform of the Russian gangster. The girl slipped into the coat. The fur was meant for a woman of a completely different breed, and the girl looked rather odd in it. Even so, she was obviously ready to make a purchase. The mobster shuffled nearby with all the grace of a bull in a china shop, pawing the wrinkled fur. It made me think of something that happened six years ago.

At that time I really wanted a fur coat, but I had only 3,000 rubles (quite a sum for those times and salaries, but still only half the price of a fur coat). One day I was standing in a little store admiring a marvelous coat made of marten, in an amazing pearl-and-coffee shade. I stood lost in thought, not even envious or sad, more filled with a kind of elegiacal sorrow that I would never have such a beautiful coat. At that moment two young girls came up to the counter, very much like the one before me now. They took out wads of bills from their pockets and were intending to buy the coat. But it was not to be. The vigilant Soviet sales-clerk, following regulations in effect at the time, demanded to see proof from the district government office that their income was legal! The girls were taken aback. How could that be? With their profession—the oldest in the world—the government didn't give out certification of income. Nevertheless they quickly exchanged glances and asked that the coat be laid away until the next day. Obviously they'd obtain the certification somehow. Why am I telling this story? Only because as I was watching the very touching scene of the couple trying on the fox jacket, I thought how, after six years, things have changed in Russia!

There I stood, a philologist with knowledge of two languages—Japanese and English—a member of the Russian Union of Journalists and the Union of Translators, a Ph.D., and yet, I was still lost in thought with that same elegiacal sorrow on the transitory nature of being, all because of the permanent absence of such a fine fur coat in my wardrobe. Meanwhile the fur coat disappeared into the dirty paws of the gangster's girlfriend, but—and here's the progress—the saleswoman wouldn't have dreamed of asking her for a certificate! (I will add that six years ago, straining every effort, I was able to buy that wretched fur coat, after publishing two or three books of my translations. Now, even if I publish 103 books, I'll have no more hope of seeing a fur coat than of seeing the back of my head.)

With the fur coat scene, my patience was exhausted. It had finally come true: the statistically average Russian citizen had absolutely no business being in the largest department store of our capital. At least the salespeople had stopped being so rude. Now they just said curtly, "Woman, step back please, don't touch the furs!" (In England and America, women are called *miss*, and in France, *madame*, but here in Russia, any female older than twenty-five is called *woman*, as if she were a biological specimen.)

The day was winding down and I headed for home,

trying out a new role for myself along the way—the house-wife consumed with the desire to feed her family with good, cheap food. When I came out of the metro station half an hour later at my "bedroom community," I saw the usual scene: a dense wall of street vendors lining the entrance and exit. Ever since January 1992, immediately after price controls were lifted, goods have been laid out right on the sidewalk, on filthy newspapers at best or on upside-down wooden crates. The selection of items has changed somewhat since then. Now the emphasis has obviously shifted to exotic fruits—bananas, lemons, oranges, kiwis, grapefruits, coconuts, mangoes, and some I don't recognize. The city has simply been flooded with these fruits, as if Moscow lay somewhere on the equator. Some are spread out on stands, and at some impromptu markets the bananas hang in bunches on a rope, as if they were dried fish. All of the vendors are middlemen who have bought from others—the fruits pass through numerous hands before reaching the buyer.

As for the other delicacies at the street markets—dubious sausages, stale cigarettes, candy and beverages whose expiration dates have passed—you would have to be suicidal to buy such things. In fact, people don't buy much, except for the fruits with thick skins—oranges, lemons, and bananas. Once I had a conversation with one of these street peddlers who was selling macaroni, cookies, and other non-perishables in packages. In the cold or broiling heat, in the rain or frost, in the piercing wind, day after day, she stood at the entrance to the metro in order to earn her pitiful 2,000 rubles (about $1), sometimes losing several times that amount because of payoffs to racketeers and the police. The price of the goods she was selling was only a little higher than at the warehouse, and almost the same as in the nearby store. Who would bother buying macaroni and cookies on the street when ten yards away was a regular store, where the same macaroni was quietly sitting on the shelf? The era of shortages was over, and people no longer needed to hunt through the city to "get their hands on" something. (During the Khrushchev and Brezhnev eras, that's the expression we used—"getting our hands on" some rare item in short supply.)

Since I never buy anything on the street (except for lemons when they're not in the stores), I boarded a bus and rode two stops to my house. Right near the bus stop is the local supermarket, of course in the peculiar Russian sense of that word.

I had to wend my way through the crowd of street vendors at the entrance. People from the Caucasian nations (Georgia, Armenia, Azerbaijan, and the Caucasian mountain areas of Russia) predominate. The selection is always the same—vegetables and exotic fruits. By evening the fruit vendors have gone, leaving behind their scraps of paper, rotten fruit, and cardboard boxes soggy from the rain.

By the store is a line of kiosks and stalls covered with all sorts of jars, bottles, and boxes in bright foreign packaging. Nobody is buying anything here, and the vendors wear expressions of terminal boredom. The expiration dates on the goods in such booths have passed not yesterday, but a year or a year and a half ago. Still, the owners of the kiosks do not seem to be concerned about selling their wares to buyers. As a rule, they have in mind a completely different purpose—laundering dirty money from all sorts of machinations, racketeering, and narcotics sales. So the goods displayed do not change for months at a time, and the vendors, languishing with ennui, are only paid to keep their mugs visible through the little window (which is not even open much of the time).

When the kiosk owners change, the booth itself changes along with the assortment of goods. You arrive in the morning and yesterday's blue aluminum booth has been replaced by an orange plastic stand, with the same yawning vendor. Only yesterday there were perhaps cigarettes, cookies, candies, and alcoholic beverages; today there are "Japanese" eyeglasses for only $9 (obviously fakes!)

Next door an avalanche of books spills over a stand —mostly mysteries, science fiction, and romance novels. There is no system at all—it's utter chaos, just like all of Russian commerce. You could kill an entire day looking for the book you want, but to no avail. There is almost no serious literature since few people are reading it now. (I remember the favorite claim of Soviet propaganda: "The USSR is the most widely read country in the world!") Nowadays books are expensive and food is even more expensive. The choice is in favor of your stomach.

I went into the market, toward the grocery section. The fruit and vegetable aisle had kiwis, tomatoes, coconuts (the most elementary staple of Russian national cooking!), some half-shriveled apples and cucumbers, and that's it. The rest of the shelves were packed with Fanta, Sprite, Coca-Cola, and other drinks consisting entirely of chemicals, but happily consumed by kids nonetheless. The only juices were orange and grapefruit. Alcoholic beverages were also available on the shelves, as they were in every section of the store.

In the next section I found bacon (with gristle for some reason), four kinds of smoked sausage (in comparison with the pre-reform days, the price is a thousand times higher, whereas salaries on the average are only a hundred times higher), ham (like nearly all meat products, imported from abroad), and boxes of frozen German pizza (we had never seen such things in the past). God knows how many times the pizza had thawed and been refrozen since its manufacture! They'd run out of cheese and milk. The fish section had frozen shrimp, unpressed sturgeon caviar, fresh trout, and chunks of salmon.

There was no meat in the meat department. To get beef or pork, you must get in line early in the morning, just as in the good old days, or else risk leaving your family without meat for dinner. The meat from the state sector is tough and tastes terrible, somewhat reminiscent of rags. (God knows what they're feeding the poor cows and pigs.) Still it's two or three times cheaper than here at the market, and safer—at least there is some sort of inspection and less of a risk that you'll buy something infected with the plague, trichinosis, or some other vile thing. Whoever is too late to buy beef can get turkey legs (imported) or pigs' tongues.

The bakery section was chock-full, something unthinkable even two years ago. There were assorted imported chocolates, four kinds of cookies, cakes, puff pastry, biscuits, candied fruits, marmalades, cocoa, five kinds of coffee, and ten kinds of tea—all imported and all very expensive. There were Russian-made goods for sale as well, but almost no one was buying them because they were so unappetizing, their packaging so depressing, and their prices not much cheaper than the imported baked goods.

There were two shelves of imported ice cream and chocolate bars—objects of lust for all Russian kids—Bounty, Snickers, Mars, Milky Way, Twix, and others. Thanks to some clever television advertising, in the last two years these brands have completely squeezed Russian chocolates out of the market. In relation to the minimum wage—and even the average wage—these candy bars are very expensive, particularly in the brandname stores. It is not even worth visiting those stores unless you have at least $30 in your pocket.

And that's it. Just as at Tamada, you can buy very delicious and expensive drinks and snacks at the local supermarket, but it is absolutely impossible to find something with which to prepare an inexpensive and tasty meal. To do this you have to go through several other stores and vegetable stands. In general, there are no inexpensive groceries for the poor, just as there is no cheap clothing, and the buyer has nothing from which to choose. Prices are such that 40 to 60 percent of the family budget has to be spent on groceries. The range of prices between the stores in the center of town and the little stands on the outskirts is not that great. The arithmetic of life is simple: If you have money, you buy groceries and other items; if you don't have money, you don't buy anything.

Of course, if you compare the current situation with the empty shelves at the end of 1991 and the old lines stretching for blocks outside of stores, then today's life might seem like paradise. But this abundance is quite relative and, moreover, it's ephemeral, like a mirage in a desert, here today, gone tomorrow. It very much depends on the political situation in the country and on the government's economic experiments. For example, after the recent imposition of new customs duties on imported foodstuffs, the shelves in the stores noticeably emptied.

The selection of food is not dictated by consumer demand but by the interests of importers, and the food that is imported is not what is most needed, but what is exotic and what is considered a delicacy. One would have a far greater chance of laying one's hands on some oysters than on some ordinary mayonnaise.

These rare items are expensive, but people pay, and they are buying quite a lot. People buy long sticks of smoked sausage and salami, which in other countries might be considered a delicacy. I know families in Moscow who gulp down whole sausages for dinner. Like my Japanese reporter friend, I too am sometimes surprised. Who, then, are the poor in Russia?

People buy these expensive items, first, because it's obvious that there are no cheap goods and never will be, and they have to eat. Second, under Russia's previous rulers they suffered so from the horrors of empty shelves and lines. Everyone tired of buying canned sprats in tomato sauce (nicknamed "unmarked graves" because it was a horrendous blob of bones and boiled eyes!). Now people want to have the "capitalist plenty" they'd heard about. Finally, people buy this food because they're afraid that when they wake up tomorrow, it will have vanished.

The abundance of food, no matter what kind, is unquestionably good. Unfortunately our food is often not of very high quality. In Russia everything that's old, outdated, or even harmful to the consumer's health is sold off. Toxic items that would be removed from sale in other countries— goods tainted by radioactive isotopes or carcinogens or steroids to stimulate growth—end up on Russian tables. Hundreds of reports about food poisoning or death have appeared on television and in the newspapers. I have never heard of anyone being punished for this. The Russian citizen is virtually defenseless in the face of the torrents of plenty falling down. The following statistics speak for themselves:

According to the results of an inspection conducted in the first quarter of this year by the State
Trade Inspection of the Russian Federation Trade
Committee, it was discovered that 71 percent of
imported alcoholic beverages, 64 percent of oils,
58 percent of cereals and sausages, 45 percent of
coffee, and 44 percent of tea do not meet the minimum standards. In total, according to incomplete
data for 1993–94, the Russian sanitary and epi-
demic agencies have banned the sale of more than
1,000 shipments of inferior imported foods, including some sent as humanitarian aid. (*Novaya
yezhednevnaya gazeta* [New Daily Newspaper],
March 31, 1994.)

I was particularly surprised by a report about a ship-
ment of canned duck pâté from some European country.
When the happy buyers opened up the cans, instead of the
pâté, they found only bare duck bones. I still wonder what
the creator of this culinary marvel was thinking. Then there's
the tea with pieces of plastic, foil, or stones in it; the rotten
chickens; the olive oil with the incredibly high lead content;
the chocolates hardened to stone and covered with white fur;
the poisonous alcohol that causes almost instantaneous death
or severe damage to the nervous system, leading to total disability. . . .

Our own Russian "poisoners"—even the government
itself—are not far behind. A significant portion of the alcoholic beverages on sale are made from industrial alcohol
and contain harmful substances such as methyl alcohol, fusel
oil, aldehydes, and esters, the concentration of which is dozens of times the permissible level. It happens that some

brands of vodka are distilled at underground plants from bioactive agents intended to strip oil from metallic and leather surfaces! The labels on these substances warn, "In case of contact with mucous membranes, flush immediately with water."

Vegetables, meat, and milk produced in Russia may contain any amount of radionuclides, nitrates, or mycotoxins. Despite a ban, medicinal antibiotics continue to be used at cattle ranches as an additive to animal feed. In a word, when we put a piece of food into our mouths, we can't even imagine what will end up in our stomachs. Russian roulette!

Still people continue to buy things. Recently the crowds on Moscow's streets have become more colorful and better dressed. Some of my foreign girlfriends have even expressed surprise after watching news reports from Russia. In your poor country, they say, the women are dressed better than in ours. How can this be so?

This turns out to be true partly because in our impoverished and unruly country people ascribe a special meaning to outward appearances, and partly because it is pointless to save rubles—inflation eats them up. Finally there is the reason given by one of my friends. Even though he is a middle-aged, very refined person, my friend reddened with embarrassment like a child when he made his admission: "I buy things, even more than I need, because I'm afraid—what if all of this disappears tomorrow?"

And that's alright, too. And it's terrible. And it's our life.

Chapter 2

Hitting Bottom

When the workday is finished and tired Russians head for home, the television screens light up in hundreds of millions of homes and Lyonya Golubkov, a national hero, appears. Lyonya Golubkov is the typical Soviet buffoon, a modern-day version of the folktale hero Ivan the Fool. Wearing a jacket and a shabby Russian fur hat with ear flaps, he is one of those people who march around the streets beneath red banners, banging empty pots and chanting "So-vi-et Un-ion!" and "Down with Yeltsin!" He's a backhoe driver, but he just as easily could be a plumber, or perhaps a loader, or an unskilled laborer, and hundreds of millions of Russian citizens follow his adventures with baited breath because Lyonya knows how to live. He has caught

The author has given this chapter the same title as Maxim Gorky's play *Na Dnye*, usually translated as "The Lower Depths."—TRANS.

the golden Firebird of Fortune* by the tail; he personifies the idiot's dream that has taken hold of all of Russia—getting rich quick.

Lyonya Golubkov is the hero of a television commercial advertising a stock investment firm called MMM, which is why he is carrying his last bit of money, crumpled in his sweaty palm, to buy some stock. "A week ago he invested 30,000 rubles, and now he has received stock worth 300,000 rubles," a velvety voice announces on the commercial. A blissful smile lights up Lyonya's face. "I'll buy my wife some boots!" he gleefully tells us. ("Well done, Lyonya!" booms the narrator's voice off-camera.)

The characters in MMM's other commercials are not to be outdone by Lyonya. Marina Sergeyevna, "a single woman, who doesn't trust anybody," *does* trust MMM. A retired man whose glasses are held together with string does too, as do some poor newly wed students. These character types have been very cleverly selected—they each represent a category of people passed over or ruined by the economic reforms. But the very same reforms that have left them behind have also given them a chance for a lucky break—or so claims the commercial. And fortune will not pass them by.

After seeing these ads, thousands of trusting souls run off the next day with their last savings clenched in their fists to purchase some MMM shares; or stock in the Olby Company, which promises its shareholders 15 percent discounts

---

* In the Russian fairy tale "Prince Ivan and the Firebird," the Firebird steals golden apples out of the tsar's garden, and the tsar offers as a reward to the son who could catch the Firebird half of his kingdom in his lifetime and the remaining half after his death.—Trans.

in the firm's stores; or shares in the Hermes Concern, which lures investors with promises of a free apartment. People pick whatever they need the most. Everyone wants new boots, German refrigerators, Japanese televisions, fur coats, cruises around Europe, villas on Cyprus, apartments in Paris, and much more, without having to lift a finger for any of it. Why do anything if you are promised what you want, at no cost and right away? If you tried to earn these things through honest labor, you'd be waiting until the end of your days.

The life of the common man is terribly removed from social scientists' theories. It is connected to these theories only to the extent that they can reflect the state of his wallet, his stomach, and his wardrobe. The typical Russian Ivan curses the economists and all their reforms because the factory where he works has been shut down for the third month in a row due to nonpayment of accounts between various enterprises, which means of course that he isn't being paid; because Ivan's wife has been fired as part of staff cuts and no one will give her a job because she's too near pension age; because his student daughter is given a stipend that is only enough to buy a bottle of vodka; because his son the ignoramus doesn't go to school and doesn't work, but just stands all day in the window of a commercial kiosk, for which he gets up to half a million rubles a month; and because Ivan's best friend from a former defense plant that used to make tanks a few years ago—the pride of the Soviet Union—is now riveting pots and pans for one and a half times less the average salary in Russia.

Meanwhile his downstairs neighbor, a petty swindler and operator, has been made the chairman of a voucher privatization fund and not only has an apartment in Moscow but one in Paris as well. Ivan hasn't gotten a damn thing from this privatization stuff, although all the local stores have been taken over either by Armenians or Azerbaijanis, who have even bought up the apartments in the buildings near the stores, so that it will be easier to jack up prices and rip people off. The whole courtyard is filled with their boxes and strewn with their garbage, but who is going to tell them off if they're from the mafia? Even the police don't get involved because they've been bribed.

Ivan's life is one worry after another: his wife's boots have worn thin and he has no money to buy new ones; there isn't enough money to give to his daughter for the school cafeteria; the price of monthly bus passes has gone up again. Ivan has already lost count of how many times the postage and telephone costs have risen, although he does know that the phone connections are so bad you can't hear your caller and that letters and packages are stolen, even though the post office skins your hide for the cost of mailing them. Ivan has long since stopped going to the barber shop because a regular haircut that used to cost 50 kopecks (with the previous average monthly salary of 150 rubles) now costs 3,500 rubles (with the current salary of 150,000 rubles—that is, if you get paid). Besides, you can catch lice at the barber's. The newspapers are always saying that Moscow has grown completely louse-infested, and that in the first quarter of 1994 alone, 1,722 carriers have been discovered.

Last year Ivan was stupid enough to privatize his state apartment, falling for the persuasive talk of those ripoff artists from the government, and now he's got nothing to do but chew on his elbows, as the Russian saying goes. It's not enough that he actually pays more in maintenance than he used to pay in rent for his nonprivatized apartment; now they're saying that soon they're going to collect some prop-

erty tax from him. Then of course there's the trouble with
his youngest son—soon the school holidays will be along,
and he has no place to go to summer camp. Ivan doesn't
have a dacha and he didn't manage to get a plot of land
through the factory in time when it was free. Now what's
he going to do? The price of land in Moscow Region has
soared to $1,000 or more per acre, and construction materials
cost as much as if they were made of gold. If he were to
send his son to one of the Pioneer camps where the kids
used to go for free, he'd have to fork over a half million
rubles for two or three weeks.

On the whole, Ivan is mad at life and the entire
world and can't even tell anymore whether he's alive or dead.
And if you add to that the problems with school and health
care, then you don't even want to go on living.

Practically every worker, collective farmer, office employee, teacher, doctor, or engineer has these problems. They
may vary slightly depending on a person's age, family composition, and social group, but the point remains the same.
These are people passed over and impoverished by the reforms, people who have lost the chance for a decent life. No,
these are not the poorest and most reviled—there are those
who are far more wretched. They won't die of hunger and
will even manage to buy some things once in a while, but the
economic reform has psychologically humiliated them, pushed
them over to the sidelines of life, and they are very bitter. It is
to these people that the MMM commercials are directed.

In January 1994, the State Statistics Committee published the basic statistical indices for Russia's standard of living for 1993. Many of the leading newspapers carried fairly
upbeat articles on the figures. I was quite surprised; it seems
we're not living so badly after all, although there are certain
problems.

For example, as I was able to discover, in some areas the fall in production has slowed, although there is no growth yet and stabilization is scarcely possible. Some branches of industry are showing improvement, but they are far from their highest level before the crisis. Spending on household consumer items has increased. But at what expense?

It turns out that the reserves are being tapped to cover these increases. This also explains what at first glance seems puzzling: even with the fall in production, the real monetary incomes of the population rose 9 percent over the previous year. There were fewer people below the poverty line in December 1993 than in January of the same year, although the figure was still 39.6 million people, more than a quarter of the population.

Prices, however, continued to multiply in 1993—9.4 times, compared to 26 times in 1992; that is, 245 times in two years. (If we recall the price hikes in 1991, prices have multiplied by 600 in three years.) The average wages have gone up 8.1 times in the last year, and 109 times in two years; that is, they have been substantially behind the rise in prices since controls were removed. But there are more goods in the stores, and 50 to 70 percent of consumer demand is satisfied.[1]

Exports exceeded imports by $16 billion (it is hard to imagine anything like this in our history), but this was achieved only by curtailing imports of grain, equipment, and medicines (by a factor of nearly four). On the other hand, the export of oil, gas, coal, and other natural resources requiring little refinement and bringing in a small profit has increased.

These fairly optimistic although quite contradictory figures gave me pause. Although I can judge economic mat-

ters only from a consumer's perspective, I once again began
to question "the good and the bad."

It is certainly an improvement that there are fewer
poor people and that consumer demand is up. But is it good
that we are eating up our reserves and not increasing production? Who decided this? Should we be so happy about
the vigorous foreign trade balance if it has been reached only
by reducing the import of necessities—equipment and medicines—and dumping natural resources on the world market? The vast depths of Russia are not a bottomless barrel,
and fewer new deposits are being discovered with each passing year. Geologists are stunned: as a result of the drastic
cutbacks in geological exploration, additional oil and con-
densed gas reserves have fallen to dangerously low levels.

Another interesting question is, where are the enormous funds gained from exporting raw materials? Whose
pockets are being lined, if a fourth of the population is still
living under the poverty level?

But the main question is, can we believe these official statistics at all? Surely we have not yet forgotten the
unconscionable falsification of production figures in the
Brezhnev "era of stagnation"! Apparently I was not the only
one concerned about this issue of the growth of the population's real income. Several publications challenged the
report, claiming it was disinformation. The official newspaper *Izvestia* hastened to clarify the real issue for the suspicious public: It turns out that the overwhelming majority
of Russians cannot believe they have begun to live better
because, first of all, inflation prevents them from doing so.
Secondly, life has changed. It has become more fluid and
more unpredictable and demands a more energetic struggle
to increase what one has. "Which actually means that the
reforms have begun to reach everyone, providing them with

more opportunities, but also placing far more demands on them."[2]

೧

Meanwhile, our television hero has prospered. In his latest commercial Lyonya has bought his wife boots and a fur coat and is now wearing a suit and sitting in a newly furnished apartment. He shows a diagram to his wife, who is nibbling chocolates: BOOTS—COAT—FURNITURE—CAR—HOUSE. "This month, we will buy a car," he says. "Next month, it'll be a house."

"In Paris?" his wife asks coquettishly. (The announcer intones, "Yes, even that is possible!")

The other characters have done no worse than Lyonya. The single woman has thrown off her threadbare fur hat and is admiring herself in the mirror of a luxuriously outfitted boudoir, pausing only long enough to run out and buy still more stock. The pensioner has packed a box of fruit and toys to send off to his grandchildren in Barnaul. The previously poor students are romping around in their new apartment—all their own! "They know how to spend their money!" adds the announcer.

These people most likely believe the State Statistics Committee's figures saying that life has greatly improved in Russia. And millions of viewers who have enviously watched the latest commercial, go to bed with a secret dream—to become just like the characters.

೧

The Russian economy is like a gigantic, uncontrollable gear set into motion by some careless hand. Three

months passed and once again we were amazed when the
State Statistics Committee released new numbers—this time
for the first quarter of 1994. I opened the newspaper one
morning to learn that now we were worse off. The tone of
official *Izvestia* was quite different. The headlines said it all:
"Russian Economy Hits Bottom."[3]

The article explained to the ordinary Russian that
this year's fall in production was much more drastic than
last year's. Industrial manufacturing had declined by 24.9
percent in comparison to the first quarter of last year, and
by 27.4 percent in March, compared with the previous
March. (The fall in production for the first quarter of 1993
was only 19.3 percent.) Our industry has not seen a situation
like this for some seventy years, since the consumer crisis of
1921–24. The government can help some factories at the expense of others, but it is powerless in the face of a crisis
affecting virtually all of them. Conversion of military to ci-
vilian production accounted for only 6 percent of the lag in
manufacturing in January and February, and about a third
of that was due to insufficient material resources. But 58
percent was caused by a lack of demand for the product!

Consumer purchases were in an even more deplora-
ble state. The volume of sales of consumer goods for the first
quarter was 4 percent lower than the previous year, and in
March, 8 percent lower. As a consequence, reserves once
again had begun to be replenished, even though the rate of
inflation had slowed.

Wages had gone up more slowly than prices but—
and here's a paradox!—the population's disposable income
had risen 10 percent. How can the average income have risen
when the average wages have fallen? Only because people
were working second jobs and making money on the side.

Statistics confirm that wage payments within the total volume of income had fallen from 65 to 59 percent, and that
the amount of extra earnings had risen.

Foreign trade was also in an alarming state, with the
imbalance in raw materials trade increasing even more. The
imposition of new customs duties on imported foodstuffs
threatened a new round of price hikes and an even larger
drop in demand. The article concluded, "It seems that the
crisis in the economy has approached what the Americans
call 'the bottom of the barrel.' "

Well, what do you know, I marveled to myself. What
economic tightrope-walking! We have become richer, although production has fallen disastrously! Does this mean
the patient is more dead than alive? It's the old hat trick
where the magician makes the rabbit disappear. Why didn't
we hear even a hint of this "bottom of the barrel" either in
January or February—or the end of March for that matter?
Surely we didn't plunge to this "bottom" in a day? And how
did we go from the "consumer boom" to such a profound
"consumer crisis" in the space of two months?

Yes, Russia is indeed a mysterious country. One of
my economist acquaintances explained that there is an enormous difference between the macroeconomic level and the
microeconomic level. The processes occurring in both spheres
are not always identical. That is, what's bad for the macro-
economy is not always so bad for ordinary people. Perhaps
that's the case, and somewhere on the peaks of the macro-
economy is an invisible clash of titans, and we only see
mountains shaking and clods of earth flying. On the other
hand, we *can* see the very bottom of the microeconomic
swamp, where it is uncomfortable, dark, and damp. Nevertheless, on the microeconomic surface, the frogs are croaking

vigorously. They were slightly squeezed in January of 1992, but they rapidly bounced back to life under the beneficial rays of abundance—the only thing that Yegor Gaidar's reforms gave them—and even leapt into furious activity. Half of Russia is eagerly looking for ways to earn money on the side—the very extra earnings that enabled the population's income to increase while average wages fell. If you earn an honest wage in one specific place, you certainly cannot buy enough to eat, much less buy your wife boots. (The exceptions are banks and joint ventures, where wages are two to three times higher than the average.)

Russians can earn money on the side by moonlighting or through "odd jobs." This usually means goldbricking in several places at once. People who have a flexible schedule and the kind of job that allows it are able to get away with this. Some manage to show up at several "jobs" in one day, receiving wages in various places for doing little. It is physically impossible to actually work so many jobs. One of my acquaintances cynically admitted to me that she works six jobs at once—and does each one badly.

This is a rather frenzied way to live and takes up a lot of time, and what's more, doesn't pay very well. Therefore it appeals mainly to people who find it important to have a certain social status (meaning the need to "be on the payroll" in some respectable institution; as a rule, this applies to all people in the arts).

For people not burdened by notions of prestige, there is a second way of earning money—through free enterprise, or trading. For example, an employee of a scientific research institute who still clings to the belief drummed into him from childhood that enterprise is shameful, is not going to sit in a booth and sell things, even for a million rubles a month (though he will eagerly cooperate with fly-by-night swindlers).

Those whose upbringing or whose desperation allows them to forget such beliefs go out on the street and sell things. Someone close to retirement age who has been fired from some office dependent on a government budget, for example, will stand under the broiling sun and pouring rain to sell a stick of sausage and a box of cookies for 2,000 to 3,000 rubles a day (about $1). Commercial stores, stalls, and flower stands are farmed out to shrewd young men and women who want to grab the brass ring without trying too hard. One can sit there the whole day, yawning and swatting flies, and make good money. A more energetic crowd buys imported consumer goods from wholesalers and sells them at retail prices. The wholesalers in turn are divided into those who deal in rubles and those who deal in dollars. Those who obtain foreign currency travel abroad to purchase the cheapest goods most in demand. These people have been nicknamed *shuttlers* because of their trips back and forth. The shuttlers do not irritate people particularly; they are not even ridiculed as black marketeers because their wares are much cheaper than what's in the stores.

The third way of making cash is by robbery, cheating, and swindling. People in this category are distinguishable from the others because, instead of selling their own wares, they sell other people's property—as a rule, the state's. In fact, it is far more prestigious and safer to steal tanks and sell them abroad than to smuggle a spare part from a factory past security—or, for that matter, to risk taking a nuclear warhead from the warehouse of a military base (although that is possible, too). Trains run all over the country carrying stolen strategic raw materials under false bills of lading, but it is rare that anyone is taken to court for this, much less jailed. A new brand of lawyer has appeared on the scene who specializes in demolishing cases at the investigation stage, before they even get to court. You can buy yourself a lot of freedom with the profits from selling tanks or oil or even shovels.

As for cheating and swindling, the stock markets, banks, and various voucher and investment funds take pride of place. With their sirenlike appeals, they lure gullible, naive people anxious to do one, quite understandable thing—hang on to their savings, which are melting like snow. By the way, how's our hero Golubkov doing? Has he grown rich or bought his house in Paris yet?

Alas . . . Lyonya didn't buy his home in Paris. And he'll never buy the cars or the furniture or even the fur coats because once again they've bilked him; all those advertisements were lies, unconscionable fraud. The shares in MMM that could be purchased everywhere were extremely hard to unload. In order to sell them, one had to sweat all day in endless lines with people just as eager to get rich quick. And if one wanted to get rid of stocks worth more than a hundred thousand rubles or so, they would most likely tell you they had run out of cash, or were closing for lunch, and it was better to come back another time because, unlike Lyonya, the people there knew how to count only too well and understood perfectly that the longer the tiny savings of the Golubkovs of the world were in their hands, the richer MMM would be. But what will happen to Lyonya? At best, he'll buy his wife those boots. At worst, he'll lose all his money. And it will be other people entirely who will go to Paris— people who are very skilled at spending other people's money.

∽

In April the newspapers published the names of the fifty most influential entrepreneurs in the country, and it turned out that at the very top of the pyramid, the highest four places were occupied by financiers and bankers. On the whole, most successful businessmen are representatives of financial capital. About a third are stockbrokers and newfangled merchants. Enormous amounts of capital have accumulated in Russia within the last few years. Russia is now a Klondike, an El Dorado, a field of miracles, where the gullible Pinnochio buries the last pieces of gold with his bare hands, succumbing to the enticements of Alisa the Fox and Bazilio the Cat.* People are stoic, patiently waiting in vain for money to start growing on trees.

What has been going on in Russia for the last two years is hard to call reform. Instead, it is a divvying up of the pie, a regrouping of the *nomenklatura*† elite who have gotten their hands on certain pieces of what was previously state property. Some have managed to grab one piece; others have latched onto another. Meanwhile the millions of Golubkovs have only the illusion of relative riches seized out of thin air, which will vanish any minute, because there is nothing of substance backing them up.

---

* From the unabridged version of the Pinnochio story. The fox and cat lured Pinnochio into a "field of miracles" promising him his money would multiply if he buried it.—Trans.

† The original *nomenklatura* in the Soviet system were the party-approved personnel in top party, state, and economic posts. The term has come to mean privileged officials of various types in Russia.—Trans.

Chapter 3

The Zone

I have a daughter, Dasha, who looks like a porcelain doll, with hair like molten platinum. She is already ten years old but I have never once risked letting her out of the house alone, not to play in the yard, nor to run to the store for a loaf of bread, nor to her girlfriend's house next door. Especially not to school, which requires a twenty-minute trolleybus ride. She is taken to school each day and afterward either her grandfather or grandmother picks her up, since I have no time to do so with my crazy work schedule. There are no school buses in Russia to pick up children and return them to their homes. I wait in terror for the day a few years from now, when she realizes that she is an independent person and demands her freedom (which she has the full right to do). I have a kind of animal fear, a nasty feeling in the pit of my stomach at the thought of someday being forced to allow this fragile, defenseless, and attractive creature out into the hostile world surrounding us. Into the *zone*.

In Russia, we've long since grown accustomed to the word *zone*, which has entered our language, our culture, our consciousness, our mentality. During the years of the Communist regime, we became used to the idea that the zone was frighteningly close, right nearby, and that anyone could wind up there. In the old days, the zone meant prisons, dungeons, labor camps, Siberia. But now the meaning of the word has expanded to include the zone of violence, fear, and lawlessness that has spread over all of Russia.

The zone of the old days was a terrible world where the lords of the underworld reigned over honest people. That zone had its own laws, and they were strict and ruthless. Even so, the zone and society existed as separate entities. Now, timid and frightened, we are all living under the laws of the zone, making our way around this kingdom of fear, with our lives, health, and wallets constantly at risk, and with an incessant, horrible feeling of humiliation.

Of course in the old days, we Russian mothers who let our children go out into the Big City were tormented by fears: What if they lost their way? What if a car hit them? How naive we were! We could never have imagined what horrors awaited us in only a few years.

You open up the newspaper—and break out in a cold sweat, reading between the lines of the police blotter in horror. Every day, as if they were given instructions, there's the same selection: two or three bombings; several domestic murders; a few mafia score-settlings (killing not only the intended victims, but innocent passersby as well); three dozen or so robberies and thefts with assault; rapes; dismembered corpses and severed heads; and savagely brutal murders committed by maniacs.

I'm especially traumatized by the column called "Wanted by Police." There are photos, one after another, showing the formless stains of corpses and the disfigured faces of those tortured and murdered. There are even the winsome little faces of children who have disappeared without a trace. The dry facts slice your heart like a razor: "Went out to visit her girlfriend and did not return. Dressed in a green sweater, boots, a short fur jacket. Anyone knowing about her whereabouts should call telephone number so-and-so." I look at the date the girl disappeared: February. Now it is already midsummer, which means they've been looking for her for half a year. Here's another one: "Child, five years old, disappeared, last seen playing in the sandbox in front of his home. Please call." Several months have passed. Where are these children now? All well and good if they are still alive—even if it's in some sort of den for juvenile prostitutes under the watchful eye of criminals. Or in the clutches of professional beggars.

I can imagine the scene: an unfortunate mother standing at the window, waiting for six months, growing gray, turning into an old lady, almost losing hope, searching every face—but still standing, looking into the distance, hoping for an incredible miracle that her child will suddenly come around the corner and say, "It's me, Mommy!" But the likelihood of a miracle is terribly small.

As I imagine this heartrending scene, I clutch my daughter's hand even tighter as I walk with her through the crowded Moscow street. Perhaps I'm a crazy mother, but I don't take my eyes off her even in the store, when she goes to a nearby counter to buy a candy bar or an ice cream cone—after all, people's children are stolen right out from under them all the time!

There was a case recently on Balaklavsky Avenue where a young woman sold a three-year-old girl for 5,000 rubles ($2.50 at the time!). She had stolen her away from her niece when the child was out walking with her half-blind grandmother. Of course it's a terrible thing, a trauma for the child's whole life. And although it's illusory, insignificant, there's still a chance that someday the mother will see her child. But what if she has been murdered? Buried in the woods, or roasted over a campfire, or chopped into bits and strewn all over Moscow's garbage heaps (and such things are known to happen these days)?

At one time, everybody in Moscow would freeze in fear when they saw an ambulance. The city was rife with rumors of a gang that had found a way to sell organs for transplants. The criminals would supposedly drag children into the ambulance by force, kill them, and immediately send their fresh blood and "donated" organs abroad through their own channels.

My hair stands on end when I think of an incident that happened recently in the very center of Moscow. Some children were playing in the courtyard of a building. A car was parked there with an empty juice carton on the hood, which for some reason was attached by a thread to the windshield wiper. Curious, one of the little boys knocked the carton to the ground, and the whole car exploded. The boy's arm was torn off and his face was turned into a bloody mess—he died instantly. The newspapers said the bomb in the juice carton was intended for the owner of the car, a small-time businessman. Who can promise you that your child won't be blown to bits by such a hidden bomb?

To tell the truth, I myself am somewhat afraid to walk the streets of Moscow, especially as it gets dark—and especially after the one evening when, around 8:30, I ran into a man, completely naked except for high-heeled shoes, who was standing in the bushes outside my building. As bad luck would have it, the electricity was out in the whole neighborhood, so there were no streetlights and people were staying indoors. I realized in despair that whether I shouted out or not, no one would hear me or come to my aid. But for some reason the maniac had mercy on me and let me go. I live on the fourteenth floor, and of course the elevator wasn't working since there wasn't any electricity, but I raced up those stairs as quick as a rabbit. Ever since, I don't go anywhere without a mace can, although I realize that when push comes to shove, it probably won't save me—it just makes me feel safer. Many of my girlfriends have armed themselves with electrical stunners.

I carry the mace can not only in the city but out to my dacha in the suburbs of Moscow. Dacha plots anywhere in Russia are typically built in a specific fashion: a dense concentration of little wooden houses surrounded by a fence or barrier against local thieves and vandals. The barrier is purely symbolic, since it has numerous gates that no one ever locks, so anyone who feels like it can come in. And that's just what the residents of nearby villages do. Burning with class hatred of the urban "bourgeois," in the winter they set fires inside, dirty the rooms, and steal furniture and refrigerators. In the summer they pinch fruit and vegetables from the gardens and lift tires and even windshields from the cars where the owners have not installed metal garages. (Until we put in such a garage, my father used to tie a rubber band with a bell to the car at night, in case thieves broke in. Although it would have been easier to install an alarm, Papa doesn't like such aggressive gadgets. He and his contraption made a scene that was as ridiculous as it was pathetic. After a sleepless night waiting to hear the bell, his blood pressure would go up, of course.) At least people aren't murdered within the confines of the fenced-in area. But beyond the fence no one can be sure of life or limb.

Just the other day there was an incident that alarmed the whole neighborhood. Our neighbor, a young man of about thirty, had guests over the weekend, several men and a girl of about twenty-five. The area is picturesque—a meadow, woods, a pretty stream, nightingales singing. The young people wanted some romance and after a pleasant picnic on a nice warm night when the moon had come out and the woods were lit with enchanting beams, the girl and our neighbor set off in the car to the stream to take a swim and listen to the trilling of the nightingales. They took a dip, listened to the birdsong and then headed home. But on the way back, the car got stuck in the mud. A campfire was burning peacefully in a field, and several local fellows were sitting around and chatting. Our neighbor went up to them and politely asked them to help pull his car out of the mud. In reply the kids beat him so brutally that he was only able to crawl home to his dacha by morning. The girl was gang-raped and the car was stolen. The young thugs, all from the nearby village, were caught the very next day and the car was found, although minus the tape deck and radio.

Fear has become an accustomed factor in our lives. We have come to endure this fear, we live with it, but nevertheless it grows constantly. When you take an airplane, there is always a risk that terrorists will hijack the plane, and the passengers will be taken as hostages. When you take the train, you expect an armed raid, especially on the southern corridors. Last winter on a train, a gang pumped narcotic gas through the doors of sleepers occupied by well-dressed passengers. Once the people were unconscious, the criminals came in and helped themselves unimpeded. It's such a cinch to open the lock from outside that sympathetic conductors pass out iron rods to the passengers at border stations, so they can additionally secure their doors from inside. One of my acquaintances, shaken, told me what he had seen with his own eyes on a train: in the middle of the night, the lock in the closed door suddenly began to spin around furiously, but since the door was blocked by the metal rod, the robbers could not get inside. Even so, the fellow was scared to death.

And what can you say about hitchhiking rides from passing cars, which is extremely dangerous, or even taking taxis, which are safer to ride before twilight? The sad statistics prove that sometimes the unlucky daredevils who take such risks at best end up in the hospital and at worst in the morgue. It's even dangerous to ride the subway late at night.

Young girls answering want ads—whether attractive offers to be a companion to an old lady for a high salary or to teach a foreign language to a child for dollars—usually find themselves in the same boat. When they arrive at the address in the ad, instead of a child or an old lady, they find a gang of young men who are looking for something quite different than a babysitter. The lucky ones manage to escape; for others, such "adventures" end in tragedy.

According to surveys, almost half of Muscovites believe their number one problem in life is the safety of their families. People are as haunted by fear for their lives as they are alarmed by the economy. All other problems pale in comparison—worry over the political situation, fear of losing a job, concern over professional success or personal life. Only 6 percent of Muscovites aren't afraid of crime and many, many people are prepared to support a platform promising improvement in public order and the living standard at the expense of democratic freedoms. It seems as if Russia is again already yearning for an "iron hand."

Some believe that crime in Russia falls into two categories. The first type is the crime of the rich, with their fancy foreign-made cars, body guards, and automatic weapons. The second type is the crime of the poor, with the inevitable vodka and kitchen knives. The law-abiding citizen who is generally far removed from the first and second types is constantly at risk from both of them. He cannot help but be affected by the rise in robberies, street murders, armed mafioso vendettas, and economic swindles, of which he is a daily victim.

The crime of the rich is attracted to areas of economic growth. These are primarily the Moscow, Leningrad, Kaliningrad, and Vladivostok regions, and the Ural Mountains area. The crime of the rich has spread through these areas like a cancerous growth. The crime of the poor is chiefly concentrated in the area of inaccessible inner Siberia and the republic of Tuva. In Moscow the most crime-ridden areas are the city center, the prestigious northwestern neighborhoods, and the working-class outlying regions to the east.

A characteristic feature of the new type of crime of the rich is mainly the increase in economic felony, shootouts on the streets, and bombs that shake the city daily. As for the crime of the poor, whoever has seen the Soviet film *Little Vera* (which was shown all over the world) has some notion of this. Typically there is a filthy, out-of-the-way town poisoned with industrial waste. A dead-end, monotonous, cheerless life. Wearisome work. The father is a hard drinker. The mother nags him. The daughter is a slut. The son is a hoodlum. The only joy in life is to buy a bottle of wine and drown your sorrows. And that's how it is every day for many years.

Until the usual drunken binge ends up in tragedy—the father grabs the kitchen knife and during a drunken quarrel stabs his son-in-law.

There are ten million alcoholics in Russia. Imagine how many crimes are committed because of alcohol! When I read the police blotter in the newspaper I'm often amazed and shocked because the reporters often manage to find something humorous in the most horrible incidents. What a phenomenal sense of humor you have to have in order to find something funny about a story like this (I quote from memory): "An alcoholic couple sat down to watch television after a fight motivated by jealousy, in which the more sober wife managed to prevail. An hour later, her spouse began to take offense. Then he took a bottle of acetone, searched his pockets for his lighter, and then approached his wife, who was nodding off in front of the television set. He sneaked up behind her, poured the acetone on her head, and when she started to wipe her eyes, he flicked the lighter. She turned into an enormous burning torch and with a wild scream fell over on the floor. The husband grew scared and hastened to douse his lifelong companion. He put out the flames, but ended up in a psychiatric hospital. The wife was taken to the emergency room."

Or another one: "A sixty-year-old son-in-law split his eighty-six-year-old mother-in-law's head with an axe." (The reporter's commentary: "Isn't it a shame to die an unnatural death at the age of eighty-six?") Yes, in the ugly world of poverty, people take each other's lives in a rather inelegant manner.

Not to say that in the world of the rich murderers always have a sophisticated touch. Seventy percent of murders these days are deliberately commissioned, one more

gripping than the next. There are even special subsets of
killers now who take out their rivals or particularly obstinate
industrialists and bankers who refuse to "cooperate" with the
underworld. It's all a gold mine for the reporters, who love
to titillate ordinary folk. For example (again I'm citing
from memory), two foreign-made cars pulled up alongside
each other at a crossroads. One drove off, and the other
remained—with the corpse of the driver, his head nearly
shot off. Moscow criminals are armed with snipers' rifles,
machine guns, grenade-launchers and TNT. Western specialists frighten us with reports that Russian gangsters have
already gained access to nuclear technology. I don't know if
that's true, but recently a man who was detained completely
by accident in the Moscow metro turned out to have enough
cesium in his briefcase to poison the entire city.

They say it's especially fashionable now to blow up
your victim right in his home, the earlier the better—4:00
or 5:00 a.m. The specialists call this a "good morning greet-
ing." Each day in Moscow, eight people are murdered, but
last year fewer than half of the premeditated murders were
solved.

Every day the newspapers flash reports of murders.
Someone killed coming out of his own doorway. . . . Killed
in his girlfriend's apartment. . . . Bombed in his own car.
. . . The list of victims is long: bankers, entrepreneurs, political
figures, major businessmen in the shadow economy, presidents of companies and joint ventures. . . . The murders run
like clockwork—documents and valuables are not touched,
and there is no hope of solving the crime. Even if there is
an investigation it comes up against a brick wall because the
witnesses refuse to talk. Obviously it's no accident: like flies,
criminals swarm around something that stinks.

~

In the old days, everything was simple: there were pickpockets, there were robbers, and there were bandits. Each had their nicknames in the underworld, and each had their "specialty"—and the corresponding article in the criminal code. But now there's some kind of organized criminal, and nobody knows what sort of animal this is. Who is a major bank official? A respectable citizen and prominent financier, or a criminal headed for jail? In the overwhelming majority of cases, he's both—pollsters claim that only 16 percent of entrepreneurs respect the law. Who is a "thief in law," the title given to the leaders of the underworld in their own code? A professional gangster or an upstanding member of society, say, the chairman of an orphans' defense foundation? Everything is mixed up in Russian society, everything is intertwined. How can this famous organized crime be battled when there isn't even an article in the criminal code to deal with it?

The Russian citizen knows more or less what the Sicilian or the Italian mafia is all about—who hasn't read Mario Puzo's *The Godfather*, or with his heart in his mouth watched the heroic adventures of the police chief on the television show *Octopus?* But the Russian mafia is a mystery. Even the word *mafia* isn't really appropriate for Russia, where everything is peculiar, incomprehensible, and unique.

In the old days, under the classic "code of honor," the man crowned "thief in law"—the "godfather"—was forbidden to have a family, engage in commerce, or even own property. Now the Russian "thieves in law" (there are several hundred of them) quite calmly mix their customary criminal activity with legal or semi-legal business, and even engage in philanthropy! They no longer keep their ill-gotten money in a sack, but in ordinary banks, foundations, and other regular institutions.

When a bank starts working for the mafia, once the claws are in, as the Russian saying goes, the whole bird is done for. Bankers give gangsters "loans" either voluntarily, knowing that they aren't going to return them anyway, or under the threat of physical reprisal. Then the payoffs from rackets are deposited in the same bank. Next the rubles are changed to dollars, and float easily across the border, say, to Swiss banks. The experts say that the Russian mafia has laundered $50 billion in Swiss banks. Obviously with that kind of money they can behave like Arab sheiks.

People talk about the long arm of the mafia. The long arm of the Russian mafia comes somewhat as a shock even to Western intelligence agencies. In late May of 1994, Russian godfathers based in Germany and Austria had a gathering in Vienna. During the intervals between their social entertainment and skiing in the Alps, the "fathers" discussed the fate of Russia. In particular, they were concerned about the "disorder" in the capital. And really, doesn't somebody have to put an end to this chaos if the police and counterintelligence in Russia themselves can't do it?

There is a famous prison in Moscow called Butyrka, a pretrial detention facility where important criminals are held. In the West, a fly couldn't get through the security at such investigative isolation cells. Perhaps a fly can't get through the Russian version either, but certainly something larger can. One day at 10:50 a.m., several underworld leaders got onto the grounds of Butyrka Prison completely unimpeded, even though they were carrying firearms. Why? Not to get their friends out from behind bars, yelling and shooting like cowboys in a Western. No, they were just coming to visit, to have a cigarette. Meanwhile, everything in the cell had been prepared for the guests. The host greeted them with a luxuriously spread banquet table, prepared by some women—God knows how *they* got in. While the first group of guests were feasting with their host, there were two dozen others loitering outside, waiting their turn to visit the cell. When the gangsters were finally arrested at the scene (I imagine by accident), none of the wardens could provide a clear explanation of how they could have gotten into the prison unnoticed in the first place.

The word *mafia* in Russia has traditionally meant some powerful groups tied to the interests of government representatives—their criminal interests, that is. The world of politics and the world of crime are hardly in opposition as it is customarily believed. They are built upon similar laws of the herd, which is why they easily overlap and share a common language.

In January *Izvestia* published excerpts from a report prepared by the Center for Analysis of Social and Economic Policy of the Russian Presidential Administration:

> The growth of organized crime, which has grafted onto the internal affairs agencies and local governments, is threatening Russia's political and economic development and creating real conditions for the coming to power of fascists. In Russia's cities and regional centers virtually all the owners of kiosks, stores, cafes, and restaurants pay bribes to gangsters. All the commodities traders and automobile importers make payoffs. Cur-

rently 70 to 80 percent of privatized enterprises and commercial banks are paying extortion fees. The gangs have their own informers everywhere among the police, traffic patrol, and banks. The gangsters have begun to extort payoffs from farmers, gardeners, and residents in rural settlements. Independent entrepreneurs have been squeezed out of some areas of business entirely. This situation in Russia is different from those in Western Europe and the United States: there, organized crime only controls "criminal" activity like prostitution, narcotics, and gambling. In Russia, organized crime controls all forms of business.

If this continues, we may possibly come to a situation like that of Latin America or Italy, when real politics is determined not by the government or the parliament but by organized crime.

What? Hasn't that happened already? Can the situation be characterized any other way when the Russian market is built on protectionism and bribes, when bureaucrats are selling off the country, when the real estate and securities markets are riddled with crime? Many of the lobbying groups in parliament are closely connected to shady business. The former parliament was unruly, uneducated, and reactionary, but the current one has the opportunity to become corrupt.

The system of *blat*, the Russian term for "connections" and protectionism, was always a characteristic feature of Russian life, an obvious component of national psychology.

Now not only is the mafia grafting onto the corrupt bureaucracy, they are poised to build a vast criminal state.

～

I like the film director Stanislav Govorukhin—his movies (his most recent is *The Great Criminal Revolution*), his books, and his dazzling, inherent, purely Russian talent. As a theoretician, he is sometimes naive, sometimes odious, but his visual technique, the artistic imagery of his work is always on the mark. He has written:

> A criminal revolution is sweeping the country. Actually, it's already nearly finished. The victory of the revolution will be the final construction of a criminal-mafia state.
>
> . . . The new government that took over the Kremlin after December 1991 is completely incredible—it has turned the country into a camp of criminals, with criminal laws and a criminal morality. Under the guise of a class of property owners, it has created a class of thieves. . . . About a year and a half ago I published an article in the magazine *Kuranty* entitled "A Country of Thieves." No one was outraged. Why be outraged—isn't it obvious? But a country of thieves is not yet a criminal-mafia state. The criminal-mafia state is the next stage.
>
> . . . The mafia doesn't like the existing order. It demands to be legalized. For that it needs elections. As soon as possible. . . . The outcome of the elections is not hard to foretell.

Money will determine everything. Since there
aren't any significant "honest" fortunes in the
country, it would seem that money from the criminal organizations will come into play.
. . . Soon, instead of this bad parliament
that infuriates everyone, we will get a parliament,
two-thirds of which will consist of people put in
by the criminal organizations, and in the president's seat will be a real, 100 percent godfather.
Yeltsin is a trumped card for them.[4]

You may not agree with the sharpness of Govorukhin's comments, you may not share his political sympathies
and antipathies, but you have to admit that some of his prog-
noses are fair—his films (and book) after all were made *before* the December 1993 elections.

I have been keeping a yellowing newspaper clipping
at home like a relic, like a historical document. After the
October 1993 events, a special correspondent of a newspaper
met with a representative of a major Russian mafia organization and asked him some questions. His article was entitled
"The Mafia Has Its Views on the Forthcoming Elections . . .
and Its Own Plans, Too." I have underlined one passage in
red pencil: "We, too, will try to nominate our own candidate
in the next elections and we think he will have a very good
chance of becoming president."[5]

~

It was obvious that we couldn't go on living like this.
The spring was wound as tight as it could be; one more twist
and it would snap, leveling everything in its path. Then the

entire mechanism of the Russian state would break into smithereens. If the president did not make the right move, someone else would do it for him—whoever took over his seat.

Then it came: the president issued a decree, verging on a declaration of a state of emergency, to combat gangsterism. Its urgent measures, which conjured up memories of Stalin's terror, had been long in the making—that was obvious from the gradual building of hysteria about crime in the press. Only for the unenlightened was the presidential decree like a bolt from the blue.

A criminal suspect (even without "reliable" information) can now be detained without a court order or an investigation for up to thirty days; police and counterintelligence agents have the right to enter and search buildings and premises of enterprises, review their financial records, and even inspect drivers and passengers on means of transportation.

The decree was signed, despite the outcries of the opposition and the democrats. Who was for and who was against it?

The State Duma (the lower chamber of the national legislature) was against it, although its initial draft crime bill was even more severe. Zhirinovsky, true to form, proposed his own eleven-point program that included initiating courts-martial, shooting gang leaders at the scene of the crime, closing the national borders, and thoroughly purging the police. Attorneys and legal scholars opposed the decree, as did liberal democrats. The people were for it. With both hands. They didn't mind violating human rights—if that human was suspected of being a criminal. The people have grown tired of putting up with crime. (More than 50 percent of those surveyed said they believed extraordinary measures were necessary to fight crime even if they violated the existing constitution.) Apparently the government understood the importance of the moment, and in order not to lose the initiative to their rivals, as happened in Belarus, they decided to stake everything and go for broke. But are there any marked cards in the deck?

The other day I overheard a rather strange conversation in the metro. Two men who looked to be standard military types were talking about the decree. One said, "It looks like they gave him the high sign. Everything's already been divvied up and grabbed. So now it's time to get rid of all the small-timers, so that they don't get underfoot. They're not going to prevent him from doing that. But who's going to touch the big fish?" The other replied, "Yeah, but there's hardly going to be less crime on the street. They'll go on raping and stealing just as they always have. Our stupid rabbits. Can you imagine how the police are upping their bribes now?"

This conversation kept ringing in my ears for a long time.

There's a nice prospect, I thought. A police state with progressively worsening street crime. Which is worse—having our soldiers wash their boots in the Indian Ocean, which is Zhirinovsky's plan, or imposing order in society with the help of a "thief in law"? It's not an easy question to answer. "Out of the frying pan, into the fire," as the proverb says.

But people believe. People always believe in something better—that's the peculiarity of human nature. Thus people are for the anti-crime decree. For twisting criminals' hands behind their backs. For twisting the screws tighter, even if it means violating the Russian Constitution. Even a little terror—excuse me, I mean extraordinary measures—is permissible to combat organized crime . . . because we're so tired, so tired to death of living in the *zone*.

Chapter 4

Fond Farewell to the Sea

Advertisements are certainly pernicious things. My eye fell on an idiotic line in a newspaper: "You only live once, so live it up in Sochi!" I don't know how, but not a month went by before I myself landed in Sochi. After the experience, I wouldn't wish my worst enemy to "live it up" in Sochi.

∾

In 1993 when Russia was deluged with rain through the entire months of May and June and through most of July, the nightmare of a lousy summer brought absolutely everyone—even the most ardent wet-weather lovers—to the point of frenzy, particularly since winter had set in very quickly, by early October.

That is why I felt like enjoying some sun, light, and sea. I was so desperate for them that despite all the dangers and the inconveniences of life now in Russia, despite the collapse and chaos, I got up my nerve to head south to the blue, blue sea. I hadn't had a real vacation for a whole nine years—since Dasha was born. If I sometimes went out to the dacha, it was always with my typewriter and a mountain of work. The thought of lying around doing nothing for even one week on a wet, sandy beach seemed so tempting.

Here Dasha suddenly spoke up for her own rights, appealing to my maternal instinct. "I'm only in your way," she wailed to me pitifully. "You go everywhere by yourself, but I'm already nine years old, and except for Moscow, I haven't seen anything, or been anywhere. . . ." Dasha was only partly right in her accusations—with her poor health, I had simply not risked taking her farther outside of Moscow than the dacha, where there were fairly comfortable conditions and a car, so that in an emergency I could bring her back to Moscow immediately. But she sobbed so pitifully, so disconsolately, that my mother's heart broke and I began to waver. After all, I thought guiltily, I really have neglected my child. I'm just a terrible mother. Fortunately, I found another such "terrible" mother, a girlfriend of mine tortured by the same guilt complex regarding her child, who she had all but abandoned because of her work.

To go on such an adventure with friends wouldn't be as risky and frightening as going by ourselves. At least I'd be able to leave my daughter with someone if I had to go out to find food or medicine.

I realize that for a Western reader my fears will seem somewhat strange. Thousands of mothers travel around the world, some even with nursing infants; I myself have seen such daring women on airplanes and trains. But many of our children are weak from birth thanks to Soviet medicine and are not fit for such adventures. Besides, life in Russia gives one little inclination to travel with children. The safety of the food is unpredictable, and sometimes it is impossible to get hold of a doctor, let alone medicine. Now, since the collapse of our once great and vast country that belonged to everyone equally, where can one go? The lyrics of a popular song of the Soviet era today sound like a bad joke: "My country is so vast / it has so many forests, fields, and rivers / I know of no other country / where a man can breathe so freely."

When I was a teenager, every year I used to go to the dunes on the Baltic coast for vacation. To this day I can visualize the golden sand; the shallow, transparent sea the color of topaz; the little amber stones intermixed with the pervasive aroma of the iodine in the bunches of green seaweed; the gentle sun; the salty wind; the smoked golden fish dripping with delicious fat—the fishermen sold it right on the beaches. Even a suntan there was different—a soft lemon color. Where is it all now? In another country, where we Russians are called pigs to our faces and plates of food are thrown in our laps—even though they extract dollars from us at the international exchange rates. No, I don't want to go to a place where they will humiliate me for my own money. I will not go until the Balts learn to behave in a civilized manner regarding ethnic issues.

What about the Crimea? It was my childhood's fairy tale, where I first saw the sea, brimming in the dawn light with little rose-colored, scuttling crabs; low tide with its shallow ripples etching rib-like stripes on the sandy ocean floor, and strange, worn pebbles. Where is it all now? In another country, where they don't care much for Russians either. Moreover, a territorial dispute between Ukraine and Russia that almost escalated into a war has just barely subsided. It was not the most suitable time or place to take a trip with a child. I have a vivid recollection of the television news coverage of vacationers being transported out of Sukhumi in battleships under a hail of bullets when the Georgian-Abkhazian war broke out. Besides, the Crimea has always been a source of intestinal infections.

The Sea of Azov? It is poisoned and polluted beyond recognition. The Aral Sea? Also in another independent republic, and you risk your life if you swim there. It is a dead sea. What about central Russia? It's the same there as the dacha outside Moscow—mosquitoes and rain, of which we're sick to death.

Altai? The Far East? It's very beautiful and exotic, but too remote (in an emergency, it would be difficult to get back quickly), and also incredibly expensive—the tickets to Magadan alone cost $1,000.

How about a cruise up the Volga? One of my friends went with her husband and adult daughter on a Volga trip, paying one and a half million rubles (about $700). She and her husband were put in the hold, and her daughter on the third deck, although they had reserved cabins next to each other. It turned out that all the best berths had been given to foreigners, as is customary in Russia—we don't especially stand on ceremony with our own kind. Well at least thanks to those same foreigners, they didn't give the passengers rotten food.

Thus, after all the discussions and the weighing of the pros and cons, we were left with two options—either a tour abroad to Cyprus, Turkey, or Bulgaria (the least expensive of those offered in the brochures), or Sochi, a resort on the Black Sea, but still within the territory of Russia.

The idea of a trip abroad was rejected virtually right away. Of course, all we really wanted to do was take off somewhere to an azure sea with white sand where coconut palms waved in the breeze and dark-skinned natives strolled by—the paradise we saw all the time in the television ads.

However, the desire to land in a tropical fairy tale died at the very first travel agency. Three gals with shifty eyes sitting in a dubious-looking basement office incoherently explained that the cost of the trip shown in the ad "wasn't exactly right." First, there was no discount for children, and besides, medical insurance and meals (except for breakfast) were not included. So the low price shown in the ad that had sounded so tempting was now ballooning to almost triple the amount. Sunny Bulgaria with its Golden Sands for $800 for two no longer seemed so hospitable. Cyprus, surrounded by white-foamed sea, or Antalia, so popular among the Russian nouveaux riches, was now costing quite a pretty penny—$1,500 not counting incidental expenses.

To be honest, I felt bad spending our small amount of hard-earned dollars (really, it was pure snobbery to throw away a thousand bucks for a week's vacation in order to tell everyone later, puffed with conceit, that we had been ABROAD!) so we were inclined toward spending our vacation in our native Russian resort town of Sochi. The ocean is the same everywhere; what is more, my girlfriend had relatives in Sochi who invited us to stay in their empty apartment while they were away in Finland, where they were planning to go any day.

This last factor tipped the scales. How proud and pleased we were with ourselves—such smart, economizing, Western-style mommies watching our family's budget. Unfortunately, with all our wise computations we forgot one small but substantive detail: the specific nature of the country where we had perforce been born and raised. And another wise truth often quoted by Margaret Thatcher: "You can get a free lunch only in a mouse trap."

We flew to Sochi without any problem. After chilly Moscow, Sochi suffocated us with its relentless sun and scorching heat. Fortunately, my friend's relatives were there to meet us in their car—and why shouldn't they when after all we were bringing their foreign passports with the Finnish visas from Moscow, saving them the heavy expense of travel to Moscow. After we handed them the passports, however, their joy at meeting us quickly faded and then was extinguished altogether. Not only did they not leave us alone in the apartment as planned, they didn't even give us an extra set of keys so that we could come inside from the beach out of the heat when they were out, rest a little, and give the children a chance to nap.

For two days we dragged ourselves around the city from morning until night like vagrants. The children, delirious with exhaustion and the terrible heat, bickered and whined constantly—begging first for ice cream, then for cold water, then for presents—and got completely out of hand. The city bristled with hostile razor-sharp vegetation like barbed wire. The sun beat down, stinging us with its burning rays. The humid air stifled our lungs. This was the Caucasus and the climate itself was clearly not suitable for us white-skinned and light-haired delicate children of the North. Even the unearthly beauty seemed malevolent. Laden with gorgeous, fluffy white and raspberry-colored blossoms of overpowering scent, the magnolia and oleander trees stealthily stretched out their snakelike branches to passersby, as if to whisper, "Come closer, smell us, we'll give you the blissful, eternal, sweet sleep of death."

On the third day the exhaustion and drafts took their

toll: all four of us got sick. My friend's child—four-year-old Sasha—came down with a temperature and was sick to his stomach, and the rest of us writhed in sheets soaked with sweat, shivering feverishly.

To top it off, we learned an interesting detail we could not have foreseen in our worst nightmares: in the last two years, my girlfriend's relatives had gone from being orthodox Communists to being no-less-zealous members of a religious sect—and not out of conviction, but for selfish reasons. In fact the trip to Finland turned out to be related to the sect's affairs, and the apartment itself had been made into a meeting house, so our presence hardly fit into the atmosphere. On the third day—just as little Sasha's temperature was soaring (the previous night our hosts had "hospitably" opened the doors to our room, and all of us, sweaty and feverish, were put in a terrible draft)—we were shown the door. These "godly" people, displaying true Christian charity Russian-style, kicked sick children out on the street.

Before leaving we unwittingly witnessed a hilarious spectacle. It was a sect meeting that we happened to hear behind closed doors in our room. A young preacher, an Armenian, spouting scientific terminology in his quaint dialect, was thundering questions at the timid old ladies. "Where do the political governments of the world go?" he roared. The old ladies, frightened, cast their eyes around the corners of the room, like D-students in a strict professor's class. Finally the hostess, apparently hearing our boisterous laughter behind the door and wishing to support the sagging reputation of her sect, squeaked out hesitatingly, "To the U.N. They are going to the U.N., to talk." "No!" thundered the preacher solemnly. "The political governments of the world are going right to Armageddon!" The old biddies quivered and fell silent; they weren't capable of imagining such a dreadful outcome.

The rest of the "prayer meeting" continued in the same spirit, interspersed with some tone-deaf bleating of hymns and some explication of the homework for the next "lesson." The meeting ended with an awful scene where the charitable aid was divvied up according to the principle of "clean" and "unclean." The aid was meant only for those who had been baptized; the other "brothers" and "sisters" got zip.

We rolled on our beds in hysterical fits of laughter, stuffing the ends of the sheets into our mouths, so as not to hurt the believers' feelings with our indecency. That is why, wandering through the broiling streets later, weighed down with children and suitcases, we were actually cheerful—if a bit hysterical. We never suspected, however, that this was far from the last surprise that the indefatigable jester Fate had prepared for us in hospitable Sochi.

The first thing we did, like true ladies (in our Soviet understanding), was head for a hotel. "Yes, we do have rooms," they told us. "But only for single occupancy. There are no cots for the children—that's impossible. Otherwise, you're welcome to stay, only you'll pay 60,000 rubles a day ($30). But keep in mind that besides the bed and a little old refrigerator there isn't anything else in the room. Air conditioner? What are you talking about? If you want an air conditioner, you have to go to the Radisson-Lazurnaya where the standard rooms are $167 a night."

After that, things only got more interesting. We decided to find out about the cost of package deals at the nearest sanitorium. In fact, many sanitoria in the glorious city of Sochi (a potential host of the Olympic Games) are literally

in ruins at the present time—like ancient Carthage. The one
we came across had crumbling walls with suspicious cracks
snaking along them, but since it did show some signs of life
and had a significant advantage—it was right near the
beach—we decided to inquire. And what did we poor pil-
grims, exhausted with yearning for a vacation, find out? The
package cost almost one and a half million rubles ($750) for
twenty days, during which we would be sickened daily with
hearty insistence, first by fish with macaroni, then by macaroni with fish.

Thus, we had two options left: either change our
tickets and go back to Moscow or, like thousands of our
fellow Russian citizens, become normal "wild" tourists; that
is, look for a room to rent somewhere, despite the dangers
inherent in such a plan. After discussing it for a time, we
decided not to submit to our fate and headed off to the bus
station where we would be able to find people willing to rent
us a room or an apartment.

At the station a dense, sweaty crowd of apartment
owners was hanging around, weary from the heat and lack
of customers. With all the social upheaval and the war in
Abkhazia, there were few vacationers and the chance of rent-
ing one's apartment was approaching zero. Thus the appearance of our colorful crew sent a shock through the
gathering of natives. They jumped and danced around us
enthusiastically, staring at our mouths, and no sooner did we
utter the magic phrase "Where can we rent a room?" then
they descended on us like an ocean tide.

The first to seize the initiative was a stout lady with
a red arm band around her upper sleeve, which for some
reason had the word "Controller" on it (the police used such
auxiliaries to control crowds). In keeping with the instinct

absorbed with our mother's milk to obey anyone in authority, we meekly followed her like rabbits to a cobra. But the crowd of other claimants to our wallets, who at first had been shocked by her brazenness, quickly recovered and pushed the lady with the arm band out of the way. After that, we were almost torn to bits. Out of the corner of my eye, I could see that my girlfriend was being "worked over" by three, hefty, thuggish-looking types. They were offering her "an apartment with your own key."

One apartment owner said, "Come with me or I'll stab you!" (That must have been what passed for humor locally, but with his jeering mug we couldn't be completely certain that his invitation wouldn't end in fatality.) It was obvious that "an apartment with your own key" would mean a quick trip to the morgue, or at best to the police station with a complaint of stolen goods. We would not be the only ones to have a copy of this much-discussed key; the felonious-looking owner would be sure to keep his. Only one option remained, taking a room from a family.

Then to my horror, I saw that two ladies had latched on to Dasha, one with pale, washed-out eyes and the other a rural-looking dame whose breasts spilled out of her sarafan, a type of flowery and shapeless Russian shift. Stepping around me, each whispered into my ear, like Scheherazade, what fantastic tempting things awaited us. It seemed that we could live at their house practically for free, with the sea right under our nose, and all the conveniences. But people from another outfit who were hanging around nearby, not to be caught napping with the competition, began to interject sobering remarks, poisoning our joy with doubt like the biblical serpent. "Hey, take a look at her, she's a drug addict!" they cried. (My God, I thought, glancing at the pale eyes of

Scheherazade, that would be the last straw!) "And look at that one in the sarafan," said the serpent, not letting up one bit. "The ocean is far away, the bushes around the house are prickly, and there's no shower! You'll be washing out of a basin!" (Out of a basin? For that kind of money? No thanks!)

The jackal-like bickering among the herd of competitors grew louder. Their eyes glowed with yellow fires, and we were grabbed and passed from hand to hand with the children silently and fearfully pressed against us. I felt waves of despair engulf me—another second and I would have given my last kopeck for a roach-infested room in a stinking hostel just to be left in peace.

Just then we were literally rescued by a nice, extremely intelligent-looking woman who, for about ten minutes, had been observing the chaotic scene of the unfortunate travelers being torn to bits. Without any request from us (God, are there really such decent people left in Russia!) she came up and politely but firmly said, "That's it. These are my acquaintances. You will bargain through me."

The crowd immediately shrank back and grew timid, forming a line to our rescuer. Within five minutes it was all over, and we were following a pleasant-looking, middle-aged woman who lived almost at the sea's edge and who charged us a mere pittance: five dollars per person per day, with children free. Furthermore we were given keys to the apartment so that we could come and go when the owners were out, and permission to use the refrigerator and kitchen with a gas stove.

The apartment turned out to be rather unusual, surprising us with its quirky mixture of pompous luxury and ugliness: an expensive stove, bathtub, and toilet, costly

Finnish appliances, mirrored ceilings—but worn scatter rugs, beat-up kitchen furniture, and tin kitchen utensils. There was an explanation for this, however. The son-in-law, who supposedly had ties to the mafia (although from their stories it was obvious that in fact he was practically the chief mafioso), had disappeared after grabbing some mafia loot, but had managed to fence all his beloved wife's valuables and even the luxurious rugs and furniture. He had even convinced his gullible spouse to sign a loan for three million rubles. The terms were such that the sum quickly grew to twice the amount—$3,000. That's why they were forced to sell the garage and the dacha and rent out the apartment so that they could somehow pay off their creditors. The apartment renters had managed to steal whatever the son-in-law hadn't sold off, and the mafia came to their house practically every day to threaten them with reprisals if they didn't give up the apartment.

Do I need to describe what inexplicable joy this brought us? Here we were under the noses of the Sochi mafia. Worse, the owners weren't home at night (the old man and his wife were out working off their "debts" at night jobs, and the daughter was working in a casino, returning home only at dawn). Still, we couldn't find lodgings a third time—especially when we couldn't tell where we might end up next! We decided to trust in God's will. So it's the mafia; we'll get along somehow.

Cheered with that thought, we decided to relax and celebrate our freedom from the religious fanatics with an evening swim. When we headed for home though, we became hopelessly lost. There is a legendary saying: "The nights in Sochi are very dark." It was true—the nights were really dark and very scary, redolent of crime. Darkness falls on the city suddenly, like a curtain dropping in the theater of the absurd, after which a pitch-black, murderous night begins. They say that there were far fewer murders in Sochi this year than in the past, but even one would be enough for us, and we weren't looking for adventures. The night life was bustling only on the main street of the city. As soon as you stepped toward a side street, you couldn't see your hand in front of your face, and there wasn't a soul about. That night it seemed that we would never get home.

Just as our desperation was reaching its peak, two suspicious males approached us, and since there was no one else around we asked them for directions. The fellows exchanged glances, whispered to each other, and then said helpfully, "Right away. We'll take you there." And they did.

But the further away they led us, the less we liked the look of it. And you can be sure we didn't like it when we came smack upon a disreputable-looking passageway through a building under construction with a pit inside. The scene was right out of the textbooks—on criminology. Realizing that it was time to get the hell out of there (we had even forgotten to bring our mace cans with us that night), we hurriedly stepped away. "Where are you going?" our helpful guides asked us in surprise. "It's right nearby." To our relief, some human figures were looming in the distance and our guides melted into the ink-black Sochi night. About forty minutes later, we finally reached the house and collapsed on our beds in utter exhaustion.

The two days after that passed in relative peace and quiet. We almost began to enjoy life. First, we found an oasis of sorts among the cigarette butts and trash on the Sochi beach—a private beach for wealthy people costing a small admission fee. For a separate but also reasonable charge you could rent an umbrella, deck chair, beach swings, and even catamarans and scutters for the whole day.

The sea was fairly clean, although sometimes you'd think you were swimming into a jelly fish and it would turn out to be a floating condom. But what would a Russian beach be without this? Everything is relative, anyway. I was shocked to discover that the blue Bosphorus was a cesspool, although the local people obviously enjoyed it.

By our Russian standards, the food was wonderful as well. The city simply overflowed with produce, drinks, juices, and other things. Everything was very tasty (especially the dairy products, some of which, like the bottled coffee milk and the sweet-sour, thick acidophilus yogurt, simply weren't made in Moscow). Food was cheaper than in the capital and, more importantly, fresher. Fortunately none of us caught any stomach ailments. The market was very well stocked and quite accessible. The produce came from nearby Turkey, the vegetables and fruits from neighboring Abkhazia, which was still at war. You got the impression that half of Abkhazia had gathered at the Sochi bazaar, but Armenians controlled most of the trade (and perhaps the entire economy of the city).

A particular danger for vacationers' wallets were the stalls, a gallery of booths arranged so cleverly that you could not avoid them on your way to and from the beach. It was like a black hole in space, dragging in the unsuspecting traveler and never releasing him from its magnetic field. There were so many temptations that someone on vacation, especially a child, simply could not resist them all. There were clothes, shoes, dishwares, and silly but endlessly amusing knick-knacks—like a backscratcher in the form of a woman's manicured hand, which gave off a dreadful noise like a belly-laugh when you used it. (All the tourists in Sochi were walking around the streets of the city like insane people, scratching with these things, and hooting and howling.) After all, Sochi is a port, and the selection here was far more varied. So with each passing day, my wallet grew slimmer while my suitcase swelled up like a leech (when I thought of the trip back home, I hatefully kicked the thing). By the end of the third day I had come to despise those booths and tried to make a big detour around them.

Alas, our idyllic happiness was not fated to last long. Perhaps the fanatics used black magic to put a hex on us, or perhaps our horoscopes were bad, but by the fourth day the nightmare had returned with a vengeance.

First little Sasha got sick. He writhed in bed with a fever for two days, his chest congested and wheezing. Finally we broke down and called the ambulance*—what if it were pneumonia? The ambulance took a rather long time to arrive, but finally did come. The doctors diagnosed his illness as a "mild cold." After they left, things got much worse. Once I found out that little Sasha was more or less alright, I decided to take some cough medicine so as not to continue bothering everyone around me with the bronchitis I had caught at the sect members' home. The medicine seemed innocent enough in appearance, a children's cough remedy, as I had been told at the kiosk where I had bought it for a very low price. "Well, if it's cheap, it can't do much harm," I reasoned, examining the label. "Poppy seed extract" it read, and that clinched it for me. Poppies are common flowers— what could be so bad about poppy seeds when we ate them

---

* It is common in Russia for an ambulance to come to one's home in the manner in which American doctors used to make house calls.—TRANS.

on rolls? So I swallowed not just one, but two tablets. Oh, what a fatal error! Soon afterward I began to die; the medicine turned out to be a drug addict's dream. I'm surprised they haven't discovered such amazing stuff. When my girlfriend came into the kitchen a few minutes later, my face had altered.

"What's wrong with you?" she asked in horror.

"I think I'm floating," I said. "There's something wrong with my head."

Everything spun around in a whirl and danced like a kaleidoscope. My throat was seized with a painful spasm and my heart shrank from some crazed fear. As before, the world lay outside the window, full of the sounds and rustles of the night, but it was no longer my world; it lay beyond the line that separated existence from nonexistence, and I was receding further and further away from that last boundary, into the depths. Dasha wailed in fright next to me, and then her squeals turned into a muffled sobbing as she ran to the bathroom and began vomiting from nervous tension. I didn't have even the strength to move a finger to calm her.

"Let's call the ambulance," my horrified girlfriend suggested.

"No," I said, my tongue moving clumsily in my mouth. "They will think that I've poisoned myself and send me to have my stomach pumped, but this is something different . . . and they might kick us out of the apartment."

Just in case, I drank a spasmolytic and as the world stopped spinning so fast before my eyes, I saw I was on the right track. It was just that my blood pressure had fallen disastrously low from these "death tablets" and my blood vessels had gone into spasms. I drank some more spasmolytic and slowly, through a gradual effort of will, I managed to drag my consciousness up from the gloomy depths into which it was trying to descend. The thought of what would happen to Dasha and my friend if things got worse kept me going. I wanted terribly to go to sleep, my eyes were simply gluing shut, but I did not allow myself to lie down. I sensed—or perhaps it merely seemed so to me in my narcotic delirium—that if my head touched the pillow, I would fall into nonexistence, from which there was no return. Ever.

Nevertheless, the nightmare that had seized me relented in about three hours and we spent the latter half of the night chatting, alternating between reminiscence and hysterical laughter. Our hysteria doubled over the funny detail that, due to nerves, my girlfriend's cheek had swollen from a boil. Dasha woke up and nervously joined the fun, but when I asked why she had become so frightened before, my daughter responded, without a shadow of a smile, "Because I thought that Mama was gone." I didn't dare ask her any more questions.

The day was spent in relative calm, collecting ourselves after the horror of the night. But that evil prankster Fate, abetted by the black magic of our sect friends, did not relent. Dasha's temperature shot up the next morning. The ambulance came right away, and after taking a look at Dasha's throat, the doctor said, "You know, with this kind of diagnosis we usually take them to the hospital." My legs buckled.

"What's wrong with her?" I asked in a strangled voice.

"Well, see for yourself."

I looked in her mouth and shuddered. Her throat was covered with pus, there was a coating of gray on her tonsils, and the telltale "butterfly" mark of diptheria was vivid.

"It's either follicular strep throat, or diphtheria," the doctor said simply.

"What should we do?"

"You have to try to scrape off the coating. If it comes off, it means it's strep throat; if not, it means it's diphtheria."

"Well, take it off," I begged her. A nurse sitting nearby who looked like an SS officer shot back viciously, "The ambulance service doesn't do that."

"Well, who does?" I said, not giving up.

"No one. No one will do it in the hospital for you either!" the SS lady advised with evident satisfaction. Obviously the sight of my maternal suffering was giving her some sadistic pleasure. "They will give her a shot of ampicillin, and that's it."

Once again I shuddered in horror.

"But she can't have that antibiotic! She's allergic, she'll go into shock immediately!"

"Who cares?" the nurse answered with her customary delicacy.

Apparently my expression was so mournful at that moment that the doctor, a woman with a kind face, took pity. Trying not to look at the nurse, who was furious, she said, "Alright. Give me some cotton, a spoon, and some kerosene. I'll do it myself."

"Why kerosene?" I asked, alarmed.

"It's an old-fashioned remedy. It's the strongest antiseptic. Anyway, there isn't anything else available."

Fortunately it turned out that Dasha didn't have diphtheria. The coating came off. The doctor gave her a few shots and her temperature immediately went down.

Without saying a word I took out a fairly large sum from my wallet and handed the money to the doctor—despite her embarrassed protestations.

"Alright, then I'll look in on you again later today," she promised, and I almost jumped for joy.

She came to visit us as a private physician for three more days—before and after work. During that time I paid her as much as she gets for a month of hard work (which is all of 100,000 rubles, or $50.) Instead of eight to ten days, she had my daughter back on her feet within three. Much more could have been paid for that, but she refused. Fortunately the Sochi drug stores carried all the medicines I needed, including the hard-to-find antibiotic that is the only one my daughter can tolerate. The doctor, whose name was Tanya, gave Dasha some shots, removed the pustules, and rubbed her throat with kerosene. On the third day when the stress had abated somewhat, we decided, like three idiots, to look at the kerosene bottle the landlady had given us. Inside was a thick layer of some suspicious substance on which wood chips and God knows what else were floating. The "kerosene" didn't smell like kerosene, but more like varnish.

"It's a good thing it wasn't mercuric chloride," the doctor joked morosely. "Whatever it was, even if it was varnish, we did cure her throat. So she'll be able to fly back to Moscow."

During the days before our departure we took care of ourselves as if we were rare vases from the Ming dynasty. Our eighteen-square-foot room with its two cots for four people began to seem remarkably like a sleeper on a long train ride. My girlfriend, the most sturdy among us, was the last to break down—her lip swelled and a fever broke out from everything we had suffered.

Nevertheless, we all safely boarded the airplane and arrived home unharmed—although by the logic of fate the motor should have fallen off our airplane, or the bottom dropped out, or terrorists seized it, or whatever other kind of adventure occur that could dog every step of a Russian traveler. Even so, we landed and safely crossed the thresholds of our own homes.

There we licked our wounds and summed up our two-week saga: No one had died, been poisoned, or had drowned—that had to be entered on the plus side of the ledger. There was cholera in the Crimea and also at the Sea of Azov. That was a plus for us as well. But vacationing abroad would have been better than Sochi and in fact not too much more expensive—a big minus. To top it off, the whole time we'd been gone there had been marvelous weather in the countryside outside of Moscow. That's when we tore out the last hairs on our head.

Poor Russian children. It's bad enough not having a vacation. But a vacation like this is no better, I thought, when I brought my Dasha for a checkup after we returned.

"Did you know you have a very emotional child, to put it mildly?" the doctor asked. "We found some major changes in her heart. No, these aren't complications from strep throat, but are solely due to nerves."

I got to thinking, if we two adult women could not lift our heads from our pillows after our bizarre vacation, what stress it must have been for our poor children, un-adapted to brutal Russian reality! For a long while after, the lyrics of a sentimental tango song resounded mockingly in my head: "The weary sun bid fond farewell to the sea / The night you said you weren't in love with me."

No, we didn't find love in Sochi, with its dark nights. Not for us nor for our children. We were grateful that de-spite all the perestroikas and reforms, a few kind people had managed to keep their humanity intact. They literally saved our lives. Thanks at least for that, city of Sochi.

Chapter 5

Through the Russian Looking Glass

"How would you like to live in Looking-glass House, Kitty? I wonder if they'd give you milk in there? Perhaps Looking-glass milk isn't good to drink. . . ."
—Lewis Carroll, *Through the Looking Glass and What Alice Found There*

When Gorbachev declared perestroika and acceleration* and asked his fellow citizens if they would like to live in the Looking-glass House of Freedom, everyone heartily and happily shouted, "Of course!"

And who wouldn't?! After barracks communism with the awful *khrushchoby* infested with bedbugs and roaches,† with equal food rations for everyone (except those who were able to steal more), including stale bread with a minuscule pat of butter as the bait in the mousetrap—after this, the capitalist paradise looked like a Garden of Eden from which the unfortunate Soviet people had been forever

---

* Acceleration, or production speed-up, was originally the second point of Gorbachev's famous program of perestroika (rebuilding), acceleration, and glasnost (openness). It was quickly forgotten when it failed to work.—Trans.

† After Premier Nikita Khrushchev who established cheap mass housing. *Khrushchoby* rhymes with *trushchoby*, the Russian word for slums.—Trans.

banished for their hideous transgressions. How badly they wanted to leave the dirt and the cold and go to where there was light, comfort, and lots to eat—to the European Home,* and to the Land of the Free and Home of the Brave. We began to think of everywhere else, where the grass was always greener—the delightful little spots on Earth of which we couldn't even dream! So we hurled ourselves into finding our secret wish, overturning everything in our path, cursing and shooting, selling our mother and our Motherland, then covering our heads with ashes and repenting, repenting, repenting, even for sins we didn't commit, just in case—anything to be allowed into the longed-for Lookingglass House. And in this insane frenzy, we forgot to ask ourselves one tiny but crucial little question: Will they give us milk there? And if they do, will it hurt us if we're not accustomed to it?

As for the cautious little English girl Alice and her kitty, meticulous scientists have long come to the alarming conclusion that looking-glass milk is not only harmful to one's health, it is mortally dangerous. Alas, it is a scientifically proven fact. In complete accordance with the laws of stereochemistry, something happens to the milk isomers in Looking-glass House so that Alice cannot even touch looking-glass milk—if she does, she'll simply explode. That is, if Alice hasn't managed to turn into anti-Alice when she gets behind the mirror.

The vast majority of yearning Russians never got behind the looking glass of freedom and prosperity, although

---

* Gorbachev was perhaps the first European statesman to begin to speak in the late 1980s of "our common European home" as a metaphor for a reunited Europe.—TRANS.

they gulped down looking-glass milk because the hand that fed them was still quite generous. To be sure, by virtue of their adaptation to all sorts of natural disasters, they didn't explode although, because they weren't accustomed to it (what went down came back up), they got social and moral indigestion. Many Russians may have missed *Through the Looking Glass and What Alice Found There* when they were children, but their mothers probably told them in their cradles the ancient Russian fairy tale about Alyonushka, a little girl who was no less intelligent than Alice. Alyonushka told her little brother Ivanushka, "Don't drink from the goat horn, you'll turn into a little goat!" But little brother Ivanushka didn't heed her warning, and drank.

Just like Ivanushka, millions of Russians turned into wretched, lousy goats, obediently swallowing the swill of anarchic pseudofreedom and phony prosperity—all because they hadn't learned the wise, eternal books, where it is written in black and white that the new is just the thoroughly forgotten old, and that before making a step forward, you should first take a look back. Or as the Russian proverb puts it, measure seven times before cutting the cloth.

Now when I see the usual fiery orator on the television screen, yelling and beating his fist against his chest, calling all the Russian goats (or rather sheep) to build democracy (the economy, statehood, law and order, whatever —the words are easily interchangeable) on the European (or American, Chinese, Polish, Japanese, German, or whatever) model, I no longer have the wish to ask, as Alice panted out to the Black Queen, "Are we nearly there?" I remember the reply only too well: "Nearly there! . . . Why, we passed it ten minutes ago!"[6]

Surrealism is interesting to me as a trend in art, not

politics. And satirical tales make me smile only when I read them while sitting in a comfortable armchair with a cup of aromatic tea. But in real life when you suddenly, and with an inevitable sense of doom, recognize yourself among the characters of Orwell's *Animal Farm*—alas! I am not such a hopeless masochist as to fall into literary ecstasy from such insights.

The filmmaker Stanislav Govorukhin wrote an article called "A Country of Thieves on the Road to the Radiant Future" which I will cite at length because it is axiomatic:

> From time to time you have to sum things up. Where have we come from, where have we got to? What have we achieved? We'll make a mental scorecard of what was and what is.
>
> The iron curtain is still in place, only now it is called the "golden curtain." Glasnost . . . glasnost is quite relative. The left-wing newspapers lie as much as the right-wing. Bribes have become larger, and graft is more widespread. Crime has long since overtaken even the post-war levels. For the first time since the war, the mortality rate has exceeded the birth rate. The public atmosphere has become even more oppressive. Culture and art are on their last legs. Theaters, studios, and publishing houses are closing. We have turned out to be unprepared for either freedom or democracy. Liberties have crushed us.
>
> Finally, people are dying. Just like before, in the cursed 1920s, 1930s, and 1940s. They are perishing in ethnic conflicts, dying of diseases for

which medicines are unavailable or from poor nu-
trition. Soon they will begin to die from despair,
from fear of the future alone. And is *that* what
we call democracy?

People steal like never before. Ninety
percent of the so-called entrepreneurs are swindlers. They're selling air. They're middlemen.
They are not building enterprises and they are not
producing. How rotten—the con men are saving
the country! We are not only a country of thieves;
we are a country of thieves and poor people. With
the enormous impoverishment there is a rapid
process of lumpenization of the country. A blind
force can be molded out of this dark, angry, dis-
oriented mass. All that is needed is a *vozhd*,* a
great leader, who will find the key to these peoples' souls. It's a Satanic time!

When the government doesn't fight
crime, two conclusions beg to be drawn. Either
they aren't capable of fighting it, or they're part
of it themselves. Both conclusions are not reas-
suring. In both cases the government itself is
criminal.[7]

I remember well the time when these lines were written. I remember Russia in January 1992, beaten down, tormented, frightened, humiliated by the puppetlike but for that
matter no less terrifying coup after the collapse of the Evil
Empire—which was, nevertheless, a great empire that gave
its inhabitants a sense of national pride. After the fall of the

---

* Stalin was referred to as the *vozhd* and Vladimir Zhirinovsky has also assumed
this title.—TRANS.

communist idea and faith in tomorrow, which in fact never brought faith in the new, Russia was almost brought to its knees, confused, desperate, angry. I remember the first weeks after price controls were lifted, when people died of heart attacks by merely looking at the price tags in the stores. An unhappy, tormented country—not a country really, but just a mass of bruises. My heart filled with pity for everything living and hatred for those who had brought my Motherland to such a brink. That winter, we Russians shouted loudly to the whole world—and we certainly know how to shout— that if we weren't helped immediately, Russians would die of hunger, cold, and epidemics. And the entire world raced to provide us with humanitarian aid, some moved by a feeling of pity and empathy, others simply by healthy pragmatism—better a living corpse, than a disintegrating, stinking one spreading infection over the globe. But much of that humanitarian aid was either stolen from the airports and never reached its intended recipients or was sold in commercial kiosks (with the sanction of the authorities!) for outrageous prices. I remember the ads in the newspapers: "Humanitarian Aid For Sale Now!" What immorality!

God alone knows where the profits from the sale of this aid went. It was reported that it went to meet the city's needs. But a city can have very, very diverse needs. For example, free lunches in charity cafeterias—are those needs? Of course, very much so. But new Mercedes for Moscow city officials—are those needs? I won't hazard a guess, because this involves the realm of relativity in physics.

Even if the aid did get to its intended recipient, it was usually pilfered anyway—with rare exceptions—by the bosses of the institution to which it had been sent. In a word it corrupted the greedy Russian citizen addicted to "looking-glass milk." I was a witness to such an incident myself. A certain institution received two enormous truckloads of produce and goods from colleagues in Germany during the winter of 1992. For two days the trucks were parked at the front steps, and for two evenings under cover of twilight after the work day there was a furious bustle of activity: the director and his cronies took things away by the boxload. Of course the director himself didn't get his hands dirty—loaders and drivers did that for him and simpler folk packed up bags and ran under cover of darkness to the metro station. Ordinary employees—and among them were quite a few who were really needy, including single mothers with several children—did not even know about the trucks. After everything had been dragged off, a "charity party" just for show was organized for the employees' kids. A table was set with sandwiches and only one glass of soft drink for each child. (The bottles were not even left opened on the table so they could serve themselves.) I don't have the words to describe politely this incident: all the appropriate lexicon would be considered vulgar.

Soon afterward there was a blessing ceremony to open a new building within this institution—that sort of thing is extremely popular now. I watched with interest as the director and his close associates bowed on cue in the Russian Orthodox manner, making huge signs of the cross over themselves. Did they remember the Ten Commandments at that moment?

∾

Going down Govorukhin's list, let us see if anything has changed in Russia. Three years have gone by after all. Are we still the same hideous, tormented, and humiliated country?

The curtain remains in place and has even grown heavier, although it is also vexingly transparent and selectively penetrable. Oh, how easy it is to see what's on the other side now! So enticing, so accessible—but not for everyone. For the chosen. For those who can indulge themselves. True—and here's the paradox!—a person who tries to earn an honest living can't indulge himself. Unfortunately the magic Looking-glass House opened its hidden doors for other people (the pigs, as Orwell would have it), for the anti-Alices who can make money out of thin air. As for all the others—the sheep, the cows and the old nags—let them look at the radiant future on their television sets, beholding with their own eyes the next installment of the endless Mexican soap opera.* Let them attach themselves to world civilization that way for the time being.

As for glasnost, freedom of speech has grown markedly restricted as journalists have come under threat. They don't romp as much as they used to, the crack reporters don't practice their wit in front of the cameras any more. They nip at the heels of the small fry, but dare not touch the big beast, especially in any vulnerable area. Otherwise they might catch a bullet in the back of their head. (There have been so many examples of that already that journalism is probably the riskiest profession.) Or perhaps a libel lawsuit of several million dollars from an indignant litigant will make their day.

Liberties are more and more restricted—rallies and marches can only be held with a permit obtained in advance from the Moscow municipal authorities, and must follow a defined route. A step to the left or right is considered escape,

* Mexican soap operas such as *The Rich Also Weep*, dubbed into Russian, have become extremely popular in Russia.—TRANS.

as the labor camp guards used to say, although given the rampant crime perhaps the measure has some grounds. Sometimes it reaches the point of absurdity, however. On May 1, the traditional Communist labor holiday, Valeriya Novodvorskaya, a famous Russian dissident against all regimes, decided to demonstrate outside Lenin's Tomb with a quite innocent sign: Communists, Take Away Your Bones! She was hauled away to the police precinct—she didn't have a permit! In front of the cameras for all to hear, the ex-vice president and ex-putschist Aleksandr Rutskoi called for the overthrow of the "antipopular regime" on May 9, the anniversary of Victory Day in World War II, as he watched a touchingly patriotic scene of burning the Russian state flag. And what of it? Nothing happened to him. He was summoned to the public prosecutor's office and scolded a little bit (it wasn't very nice to burn flags, now, was it?). After, his explanations were graciously heard. From now on he would only attempt to overthrow the regime by peaceful methods.

What can be said about culture and art? Everyone who can is fleeing—performers, artists, and writers. To be sure, even over there, behind the "curtain," it's not a bowl of cherries for everyone. Recently there was an interview on television with one of our former movie stars who went to America. She used to be great, better than anyone else, something special, languorous and slender, in wide-brimmed hats à la Vera Kholodnaya, all thrilling and seductive. But now? An old lady grown fat and flabby, her jowls hanging, her eyes dull, wearing some silly jacket—and filmed in a kitchen! A cook, with a rapacious longing in her eyes. She never learned English, she's not making any movies, and doesn't have any parts in plays. Nowadays her life is at the stove and the washing machine. She didn't throw it all away for the sake of her children, but for her own sake, and she miscalculated.

Many people—even more talented individuals of sturdier stuff, especially those who made up the first wave of emigration after the revolution—were just as mistaken. They often found life as emigrés unbearable. Marina Tsvetayeva, a poet of genius who lived abroad for a number of years, wrote:

> *A ruse—homesickness!*
> *Long ago exposed*
> *I could not care less*
> *Where I'm all alone*
>
> *Along which cobblestones*
> *With shopping bag I trudge a line*
> *Like a hospital or barracks—home*
> *A house that doesn't know it's mine*
>
> *Any home to me is strange, all churches bare*
> *It doesn't matter anymore, I do not care*

Tsvetayeva was trying to persuade herself—and others who had ended up in such pain and trouble—that home and homesickness were illusions. But suddenly, like a death knell, like a heartrending cry of despair, like an animal howl of grief, come the last lines, which nullify the preceding ones:

> *But if I see along the road*
> *A berry bush, especially rowan . . .* *

---

* The rowan is a small deciduous tree, native to Europe, having clusters of reddish berries. To Tsvetayeva, these berries symbolized Russia.—TRANS.

Artists, writers, and performers are pieces of their country, their people. Only the fortunate ones able to adapt found happiness *over there*. Isolated cases. Others, even those who are getting along financially, start to wilt without their native environment, like a flower without water, whatever they might say. Even so, they are drawn back and will always be drawn. Obviously we're made that way. Sometimes to our own peril, as was the case with Marina Tsvetayeva, once again alien and not understood in the new socialist homeland.*

It's the same now. There behind the curtain, our geniuses and our idols are at best exotic or amusing and at worst boring. But here in a Russia with a broken spine, who needs them? Where is it now, that "most widely read country in the world"? Science fiction and mystery novels have already palled now that our life itself is a fantastic superthriller. Now people have flung themselves into romance novels. What will we read when love grows wearisome? The culture of the masses and the culture of the dying intelligentsia are two currents flowing in one river bed, never intermingling. This phenomenon can be seen in some Russian rivers. The clean water repels the filthy current, and the dirty water does not absorb the unpolluted stream. Except that the clean rivulets are growing thinner and weaker. Soon we'll turn around and they'll have vanished completely.

And what of morality in Russia? It's total prostitution, from top to bottom: from the schoolgirl to the politician in the highest offices of the government. Who is the hero in the public's favorite movies? The thief, the prostitute, the

---

* Tsvetayeva committed suicide in 1941 after having returned to Russia in 1939 from exile.—TRANS.

cheat, the bandit, the villain, the murderer. Film and literature have romanticized gangsters. Honor, conscience, sympathy, loyalty—what are they worth now? Statistics show that 40 percent of wives cheat on their husbands and 60 percent of husbands cheat on their wives. And what percentage of bureaucrats and politicians (not to mention businessmen) cheat their country and their people? Ninety? One hundred? The easiest and most reliable way to earn money is to sell whatever and whomever—your country, friend, wife, daughter, yourself—just as long as the client is willing to pay top dollar.

What about the old folks and the children? Just as before, nobody needs them. We, the entire country, are living at our parents' and children's expense now. We will eat up what we should be leaving for them. Old folks are dying not just from illnesses and the shortage of medicines (or their costliness) but from despair. In fact, not only elderly people but young men and women full of strength are dying—at their own hand. In the last two years, the country has lost about 100,000 human lives to suicide (and for every actual suicide there are seven to ten failed attempts!). Why? The fear of being left without work, the shame of poverty, and the inability to endure the violent death of relatives. Some just want to get away from the mafia's persecution.

And the swindlers? They go on stealing just as before. Only their numbers have grown—the government is still competing with them to see who can steal faster.

The country is becoming an unfavorable and even dangerous habitat for life. In the last year alone the population has decreased by 300,000 people. Particularly disastrous is the situation in Central Russia where quite young people, especially able-bodied men, full of vigor, are dying. Infant and child mortality rates, already high, continue to climb.

∿

Yes, a gulp of unaccustomed looking-glass freedom played a nasty trick on Russia. We should be glad that we found what we were looking for—but the pile of gold turned into filthy broken shards in our hands.

What does this mean, that Russia is now lying in ruins, having drunk its fill of poisoned looking-glass milk? Hardly. No wonder there's an apt Russian proverb for this case: "For some it's war, but for others it's their own dear mother." ("One man's meat is another man's poison.")

Russia is an amazing country, a black box where all laws considered just by the rest of the world are turned upside down. Russia reminds me of an old-fashioned toy, *vanka-vstanka*, a kind of little doll with a lead weight inside the bottom. No matter how you rock it back and forth and tip it over on its side, it keeps springing back up—here I am!

Russia has been put through worse crises than these in all the dark ages of its existence—and each time the country rose up again, literally from the ashes, moved by incomprehensible reserves. True, each time Russia rose in a new incarnation, terrifying the unaccustomed civilized world. Even now, this cursed, trampled, reviled, and raped country has not died or been killed or even exploded. With the elusive mutability of a chameleon it has turned into something alien, fundamentally contradictory to its former self—a kind of hideous, deformed anti-Russia. At least, this process is under way, and who's to know, perhaps the world will yet be amazed by the new Russia.

The rest of the world is a looking-glass wonder for us, yet we, too, are a mysterious Russian looking-glass world. Let us look at Russia from that other side. What would Alice see through the Russian looking glass?

∾

> *"Well, in our country," said Alice, still panting a little, "you'd generally get to somewhere else—if you ran very fast for a long time, as we've been doing."*
>
> *"A slow sort of country!" said the Queen. "Now, here, you see, it takes all the running you can do, to keep in the same place. If you want to get somewhere else, you must run at least twice as fast as that!"*
>
> *—Through the Looking Glass*

In the old days, everything was clear. In prerevolutionary Russia, there were estates in society. Then it turned out there were classes. After the October Revolution, the capitalist class (the exploiters, of course) was liquidated, and the proletariat-hegemon was all that remained in Russia, along with the cooperative peasantry and the "people's" intelligentsia, which after long reflection, was classified as a "stratum" of society. (There couldn't be any classes in the Marxist society!) This was an ideal, socially homogenous society of universal equality with the distinctions among everyone erased in the process of development. It was quite unstable, but it was at least understandable. But now? As Tolstoy wrote in *Anna Karenina*, "Everything had gone wrong in the Oblonsky household."[8]

It is very hard to analyze and make classifications when society is in such a state of social chaos. In point of fact, it is not only impossible to categorize society by classes, but even by segments, social groups, or professions. These constantly overlap and shift, growing larger or smaller due to the endlessly migrating marginals and workers in a monstrous whirlpool. How, for example, can you categorize an engineer who shuttles back and forth to Turkey buying cheap junk to resell? What about a government official who also manages a firm or a commercial bank—is he a state employee, a financier, a businessman, or a mafioso? The chief sign of the lumpen is the loss of a professional code of honor. But what code of honor can we speak about when a person moonlights at three or four no-show jobs at once? So we're all becoming lumpens—the whole country—with a fundamentally lumpenized consciousness and a broken psychology.

Rather than try to classify and summarize what doesn't exist, I would like to talk about several social categories that can be found in our country—the new rich and the new Russian intelligentsia—and about the future of youth, children, old people, and social outcasts. The current state of these groups is a good indication of the overall character of Russian society.

The "new Russians," as they are called, are perhaps the most colorful social group in the country today, perhaps the most visible to the eye of the researcher, sociologist, historian, or journalist. They can't hide from statistics (or hired murderers or the tax inspectors), although some of them know how to run very fast—so fast that they manage, unlike the rest of their slow fellow citizens, to get away to their own villa on the French Riviera or an apartment in Paris or Cyprus, or Majorca or Miami. Although from time to time they experience some unpleasantness (they are shot at or blown up in their cars), the more lively the process of plundering Russia the freer and easier they run, these new Russians.

Our new rich folks are filling the most fashionable hotels of Europe, Asia, and America, spending huge fortunes at casinos, throwing money around left and right, buying priceless fur coats, diamonds, real estate, and firms abroad. They are the favorite clients of the hotel porters, who affectionately call them the "sheiks from the North." By the most modest estimates, they have laundered $50 billion in Swiss banks, remaining uncivilized natives of the steppes nevertheless. The new Russians dress in Cardin suits, with mouths full of gold crowns, but they speak Russian with the stresses in the wrong place and write with spelling errors. They buy Rolls Royces to ride to the same place they would have gone in a Russian-made Zaporozhets—over to the next village (yet they can't understand the English on the buttons and switches on the dashboard). They order designer apartments consisting only of a pool, bedroom, and kitchen, then buy expensive seasoned oak furniture and have it painted white. The new Russians spend money recklessly, drinking rare wines like bottles of juice, and cavorting on television programs for rich people of howlingly bad taste that make ordinary folks just plain mad.

The new Russians keep real harems of guarded hostages and turn their own wives into slaves. Their children go to private schools in bullet-proof automobiles, eat only organic food, and get $100 a day for pocket money. The new Russians are attractive and loathsome, majestic and ridiculous. Like hyenas, they tear to bits the body of Russia, which is still alive, but they also contrive to keep Russia's gasping economy afloat. Who are they—and from whence do they come crashing down on our heads?

It was all different with the Russian merchants and industrial magnates of past centuries. Back then, strong, solid fortunes were built up from generation to generation through persistent, although not always crystal-pure, work. Such fortunes were forged along with the glory and honor of the family name. Nowadays, however, fortunes are like one-day butterflies emerging from thin air. Yesterday's despised little crook has become a millionaire. It's right out of the American dream.

The new Russians have reached their latter-day Olympus via many diverse paths. Here you will find Communist Party money snatched up in the nick of time by nimble fingers; and income from machinations with raw materials (particularly those involving allocation of quotas and export licenses), deals with voucher funds and securities, and Western credits that end up sticking to dirty hands (it is believed that at least one third of the loans to Russia have gone astray, bypassing the intended recipients). Then there are earnings from racketeering, prostitution, and the sale of narcotics and weapons, and money hidden from the tax authorities. A very small—triflingly small—number of the new fortunes were raised honestly.

Among the new rich there are quite a few familiar faces. For example, I happened to hear over the radio that Nikolai Ryzhkov, Gorbachev's former prime minister (to whom Gorbachev, out of pity for Ryzhkov's poverty, had bequeathed his government dacha when he retired), until recently had been the chairman of a major bank. Ryzhkov's first deputy is the president of an international fund to promote foreign investments. The former first secretary of the Sverdlovsk Regional Party Committee is now the director of the State Investment Company. The former minister of the coal industry (removed in his day for supporting the August 1991 coup plotters) is now the chairman of the board of another major bank. Fate has been kind even to ex-President Gorby himself. No, we can't say the new Russian business elite emerged from ashes.

The *nomenklatura* were the first to get their bearings under the reforms. Following their lead were the "red directors," the heads of state-subsidized factories, the new Russian monopolists. Perestroika and the reforms turned them into true autocrats, the full-fledged owners of their own enterprises.

The third group consists of private businessmen—directors of commercial banks, firms, joint ventures, and commodities exchanges. These people at least started their own businesses themselves. Finally, there are the former black-market dealers in the shadow economy—the people who only a few years ago were considered mafiosi and criminals and who are now the leading figures in Russian society. How many millionaires have grown out of those schemers large and small with their bulldoglike tenacity!

I once knew a millionaire (perhaps he's already a billionaire?) who, when he was my neighbor during the Brezhnev "era of stagnation," was involved in some questionable deals related to tourism. When the saga of privatization began, he landed on his feet and now he is the chairman of one of the largest voucher funds. To be sure, his true nature, strictly amoral, shone through even in those long-ago days. I remember a terrible incident in which he sent his wife off for an operation and brought home a young girl to entertain. Meanwhile for some reason his wife wasn't operated on that day and returned home. But she wasn't able to get into the apartment: her husband ordered her to wait on the stairway until he was free. And he was "busy" for quite a while—three hours or so. All that time the poor woman shed bitter tears, sitting on the filthy steps. They didn't get a divorce, however. I don't think she'd divorce him even now, although his moral character has hardly improved—such fantastic wealth is too alluring.

Recently I happened to see him on television. The subject was the usual scam—some voucher fund had collapsed. Well-groomed, well-fed, smug, he was obviously prospering. A cynical smile played on his lips. "Of course I feel sorry for people who have lost money, but what can you do? Those are the laws of wild capitalism." I was shaken. What kind of capitalism is that, I felt like screaming. It's beyond the limit—predatory, lawless behavior, and the abuse of the gullible. If you can allow yourself to get rich at the expense of the naive and inexperienced, already deceived by the government, you shouldn't scoff at them so!

∾

Under Soviet rule, it was the intelligentsia—and hardly the Communist Party, as official ideology claimed— that was the "honor, conscience and reason of the people." The intelligentsia was the conscience of a great and exhausted country, ruled by tyrants from time immemorial. It was the beacon of freedom in a nation taught to live on its knees. No wonder the theoreticians of communism never managed to squeeze the intelligentsia into a single class—it remained a layer, a segment unto itself. For many centuries it played a special role in the spiritual life of Russia—its angel, its sacrificial lamb, deliberately giving itself up to the slaughter for the sake of the triumph of good and justice.

The world is used to seeing the intelligentsia in the works of the classic Russian writers—not always headstrong and determined, but full of human dignity, rejecting lackeydom and slavery, living according to conscience. All of us, including my generation, grew up on this soil; we absorbed the spirit of the freedom-loving poetry of Pushkin and Lermontov, and the humanism of Tolstoy, Chekhov, and Dostoyevsky.

My grandmother on my mother's side was born and raised in the North in the large family of a schoolteacher. Her father died of consumption very early on, but the tsarist government educated all the children for free, and my grandmother managed to finish grammar school. She often used to say that in terms of their high level of erudition and spiritual commitment, the rural intelligentsia of those days was in no way inferior to the urban intelligentsia. The intelligentsia itself was not a separate segment of society—noblemen, petty bourgeois, and educated craftsmen could all be members of the intelligentsia, so that this concept had more to do with the spirit and the condition of one's soul.

The Russian intelligentsia began to dig its own grave when it accepted and believed in the justice of the revolution. Betraying itself, it began gradually to sink into infamy. Moreover with the monstrous stew boiling in Russia in that time of troubles, a stream of marginals began to flow into the intelligentsia, which had previously been based largely on family heritage. These people brought in their own rules and views and were prepared for any alliance—for the sake of survival. Essentially, they were considered intelligentsia only because of the education they had received.

A brief flash of the former spirit occurred during Khrushchev's Thaw in the 1960s, but even that was enough to last through three more decades of vegetation. Then spirituality began to fade during the Brezhnev years until it was extinguished altogether during the current period of "reform." Glasnost buried it under the weight of guilt. In an effort to cleanse itself from the years of living on its knees, Russia's intelligentsia threw itself into perestroika as into a maelstrom.

Whoever cuts off the past is doomed to lose his way in the gloom of the future. By repudiating its bitter experience, the intelligentsia made the same old mistake—it once again believed unconditionally in renewal. And just as before, some of the most obedient members of the intelligentsia were selected by the powers-that-be and taken aboard the boat. The rest who clung to the sides had their fingers stepped on.

It's strange, isn't it? In the years of stagnation when the KGB roved everywhere and you got a few years in jail for telling a political joke, we fearlessly gathered in cramped kitchens and gave fiery anti-Soviet speeches. Now everyone is silent. Either they are tired of shouting or they no longer know what to shout. Only when it comes to wages do people scream, becoming active for a brief time. The creative intelligentsia, on the other hand, keeps entirely silent, letting off some bubbles and grabbing at the straw of pure art. Only a small minority of such people in the arts are prospering— those who gained access to the dollar trough. The rest are vegetating.

I know a Ph.D. in science, a member of the journalists', the writers', and the translators' unions, a senior scientific researcher at a leading Moscow institute, who receives a salary of $60 per month. This man wrote his Ph.D. thesis in his bathroom, crouching by the toilet while his whole family slept because there was no other place for him in their tiny apartment. Neither perestroika nor the "reform" has changed anything in his life—except for the worse.

The salaries of doctors and social service workers and those in culture, art, and education are one-and-a-half to two times lower than those in industry and frequently even lower than the minimum standard of living. Yet no one is really outraged by this. I keep trying to understand the reasons for such submissiveness to one's fate, for such inclination toward meekness. After all, the willingness to put one's neck under the jackboot and the readiness to sell oneself for a profit are two sides of the same coin. Where is that freedom-loving and proud spirit of the former Russian intelligentsia? Or has the inveterate fear of bloody persecution eaten into the skin?

The current times have split the body of the intelligentsia. The crack originated at a sore point, the attitude toward reforms. The creative intelligentsia, which had acquired a certain freedom of speech, although not fully enjoyed, is supporting "reform" for the time being. Or to be more precise, realizing that this is no reform at all, it simply supports the very idea of moving forward—although it does not understand the destination, exactly. The technical intelligentsia, which has lost absolutely everything, even its self-respect, hates the current government fiercely (can an engineer and father respect himself when he is unable to feed his family?).

The second fault line in the intelligentsia runs through another painful point—the opportunity to earn dollars. The life of those who earn even $100 a month is substantially different from those who cannot earn dollars. Paradoxically in Russia, a much greater sum of dollars than rubles is paid for equal work (when calculated at the current exchange rate).

Where is the Russian intelligentsia headed? Will it

take the route of meekness and slavery? Will it further divide into segments? The people could not care less. Three times Russia renounced its intelligentsia, the conscience and reason of the country: in 1917, in the years of the Stalinist terror, and now—for the last time. Because in the larger scheme of things the intelligentsia could not care less about the people. The conscience and reason of Russia is slumbering. And each one of the intelligentsia is dying in solitude.

∾

Children and old people are indicators of the health of society. When I travel to Japan, or for that matter to any prosperous country in the world, I am inevitably seized by an acute feeling of envy—not because of the profusion of goods on the store shelves or because of the advanced level of technology or the high standard of living—but because I see how the old people and children live in peace and safety. Countries that are so concerned about their old and young have a future. And I think bitterly of Russia.

Oh, Russia, Russia, you giant meat grinder chopping up people's lives. Do you remember how in the 1920s and 1930s you bred monsters who denounced their parents in the name of the state, teaching them from childhood how to betray their father and mother for the triumph of the dictatorship of the proletariat—that grand achievement? There was even a national hero, Pavlik Morozov, who informed on his relatives. His father was killed. For half a century schools and Pioneer clubs were named after Pavlik.

Do you remember how you told us the story of kind Uncle Lenin, a keen hunter, friend of little children, and a great defender of all the unfortunate? How you raised us in

reverent love for the Father of the People—the great Stalin?
And how during the spring flood, kind Uncle Lenin beat to
death with his keen oar dozens of poor rabbits who were
dying on a flooded island? With the same zeal he shot
thousands of supporters of the White idea* and all those who
got in the way of his half-mad plans. By the way, concentration camps first appeared under Lenin. And as for Stalin,
the Father of the People who covered the country with
blood, there is nothing left to be said.

In the old days, we were taught from our mother's
knee that stealing and trading were shameful, and that we
should "study, study, and study, as the great Lenin advised
us." Now it turns out that it is indecent to be poor and
honest, stupid to earn an honest living, and prestigious to
steal and trade. As for studies—that's just a way to kill time
for the hopeless. Now it's all backwards, inside out—and
that is why it is a Looking-glass House. Our poor children!
What a muddle they must have in their weak, undeveloped
minds if there is such complete chaos in our adult heads.

Khrushchev promised us that we would live under
Communism in the next generation. Now they are telling us
that the current generation will live under gangsterism. Because the great reform is underway and our very busy government just doesn't have time for children and old people.
So they'll just have to be patient, the good life will come
tomorrow. It's the old story. As the Black Queen said to
Alice, "Jam tomorrow! And only tomorrow! Tomorrow
never comes today!"

What conclusion do smart people draw? If they want

* The anti-Bolshevik beliefs of the Whites, who opposed the Reds (the Communists) in the Russian civil war.—TRANS.

jam today, there's only one thing left to do—grab it yourself, either through your papa and mama, or by your own hands. Whichever is your destiny.

Unfortunately, children do not choose their parents —nor their Motherland. Adults can choose and plan to have or not to have children. But children are just born and grow up regardless of anything. In the first two years they are almost all alike—except some perhaps have better-quality diapers or tastier food. There seems to be complete equality in everything else—but that's only at first glance.

Starting at about age two-and-a-half to three, the picture changes drastically just as soon as the child learns to run fast and babble animatedly, and to show signs of intelligence. Here it turns out that not only will everyone have a very different life, but a very distinct future—from the outset, almost with karmic predetermination, because the starting lines are different from the very beginning.

Even if they are hopeless cretins, the children of rich parents (those who can move swiftly and get into the new *nomenklatura* or business elite or mafia organizations, or those others fast enough on their feet to earn more than $500 per month) go to the finest schools. When they get older, they vacation in Cyprus, Majorca, Turkey, the Bahamas, or other exotic spots, and then settle down and complete their educations at Harvard, Oxford, or the Sorbonne, emerging well-armed and fully prepared for life and battle. True, no special struggle is envisioned because these privileged kids will already have a cozy spot in daddy's firm or at a bank.

Kids with parents who are a rank lower, but still well-to-do, have a simpler, but not bad, lifestyle. If they don't have the private lycee, than at least there's the fine Soviet-era traditional special school where children are taught foreign languages from the primary grades, plus music, computers, karate, ballroom dancing, drawing, photography, drama—all sorts of fascinating lessons. They aren't taken abroad on vacation—the price is a bit steep, after all—but their families have their own dachas and perhaps can provide them with a trip to the Black Sea. Almost daily they are given expensive foreign candy and the dream of all Soviet kids—chocolate eggs with a surprise inside. Although they aren't given their allowances in dollars, their parents try to provide them with everything—even at the cost of their own poor diet and lack of sleep. It's as if they're saying, we didn't come to town on a load of hay; our children can study ballet at home and we can pay insane prices for tennis lessons. Such families often have financial incentives for good grades in school and fines for bad ones (they have to give the child money anyway; let him at least learn its value). And of course they take their kids back and forth to school from door to door—some in their own cars, some on public transportation.

Prosperous children are "made" from childhood. Almost before they're out of diapers they know just what their parents are going to bring them on a silver platter when they grow up. Actresses and singers drag their children onto the stage, taking them from show to show, concert to concert, even if they happen to be tone-deaf. Ballerinas and dancers push their kids into various international competitions and foreign tours. Before you know it, they've performed once, turned in front of a camera, and—voila—a star by nineteen years of age! Their abilities are mediocre at best and their looks are nothing to write home about. But exposure is a great thing.

In the old days only the Party elite could indulge in

such practices so there were more chances for gifted children from humble families. Now there are more parents with money and connections and the talented kids from the poor families must make way. Now a child would have to be a genius to get ahead without money or clout—that is, of course, unless some sponsor discovers and begins to mold a "pro" out of the young genius. The Pioneer Palaces where in Soviet days the young gifted children could be discovered, are starting to die out, replaced by all sorts of neighborhood clubs that cost money—although the quality of training in them has not improved. (I took my daughter to such a place for a year, but it was a waste of time. Then I took her to a professional ballerina for reasonably priced lessons and within several months she had turned angular and awkward Dasha into a completely different child.)

What is left for the children of poor parents who barely have enough money to dress, shoe, and feed their kids? They have to send them to the abominable local schools where the kids beat each other up in the toilets and smoke pot (to be fair, even among these ordinary district schools occasionally a decent one is found). The courtyards are spittle-covered asphalt with sandboxes where dogs poop and drunks throw their bottles. These children don't play tennis or ride horseback and don't study computers and karate; they learn of life in its natural courtyard form, in the struggle for survival. These are street kids, "flowers of asphalt," and they come to an early understanding that the world essentially doesn't care about them. Neither the government nor, in the final analysis, even their parents care about them, afflicted as they are with their cheerless jobs and frequent bouts of drunkenness. They know that if they don't snatch something from life themselves, no one is going to

give it to them as a present. They are very cynical—no taboos or psychological inhibitions exist for them. They are not
afraid of the authorities or the police because they know
perfectly well that until they turn fourteen, there is no threat
of punishment for committing a crime. The new Law on Education has done them a dis-
service; now schools have the right to rid themselves of dif-
ficult adolescents by expelling them at the age of fourteen.
Where do they go after that? One after another of the trade
schools are closing, so these kids end up on the street as hired
muscle for the mafia. A third of juvenile criminals come
from poor families. Half of them are from broken homes.
Now one in every three teenagers in Russia is earning his
own living by begging, washing cars, reselling gasoline or
newspapers, blackmailing and racketeering their school-
mates, and by prostitution. Sometimes they perform small
favors for the big mafiosi. Sometimes they deal on the black
market.

Juvenile crime has risen now to the level it was at in
the 1920s. But those were the years of destruction, when the
war had left many children orphaned or neglected. Now
many of them are running away from home and ending up
in the clutches of criminal gangs. For example, when the
kids are washing cars, they usually have a lookout who's a
bit older—just try and refuse to have your windshield wiped
and they'll either beat you or break your window with an
iron rod. There was a whole gang operating around the
McDonalds on the Arbat—adult criminals in cahoots with
juvenile delinquents. They would guard cars for a payoff,
rip off things carelessly left in automobiles, and intimidate
other teenagers into joining their gang. These kids are angry
and even more brutal than adults. I recently read a terrible

article in the paper about a fourteen-year-old student characterized quite positively in his school ("a diligent, model student") who lured an eight-year-old neighbor onto the roof of a high-rise and slashed his throat with a kitchen knife. Then he demanded $3,000 from the parents for the corpse of the murdered child. To prove the seriousness of his intentions he cut off the dead boy's ears and sent them to the parents in the mail.

Specialists believe that adolescent crime is a fanatical revenge against society for the child's degraded position. It is shameful to be poor. Children cannot forgive their parents and society for the humiliation they experience when they pass by stores full of expensive goods and see the arrogant, self-satisfied mugs of the nouveaux riches. The petty hooligans that grow out of these humiliated children are ripe for crime. Now the power of the hooligan is spreading over the whole country, wielded by the mafia.

Television plays a significant role in the growth of juvenile crime, as does all of mass culture with its cult of violence. The mass media is an ideal mechanism for raising all sorts of maniacs, sadists, and perverts. Children playing on the street pretend they're Freddy Krueger from *Nightmare on Elm Street*, sticking nails in their gloves for claws.

Little girls are not far behind boys in their sadism. There have been cases where girls have kicked drunks to death on the street in order to rob them. ("My mama sent me out to earn a living.") They also sell themselves, performing oral sex right in cars, toilets, and cellars for 5,000 rubles ($2.50). And that's at ten to twelve years of age! Sometimes the mommies themselves hawk their daughters' charms— but then the stakes are higher and greater sums are paid.

There is another particularly terrible category of

children—the train-station kids. They live in the waiting rooms, drinking, smoking pot, playing cards, earning a little money, and enjoying the video games. These are children who have run away from their troubled homes.

An even more monstrous variation are the *bomzhi** children of vagrants who are taken along by adults to beg. Some have been kidnapped and some are the beggars' own children, but they are all physically underdeveloped and psychologically crippled, children lost to society. The infant *bomzhi* sleep quite soundly in their "mothers' " arms because they've been sedated. The older ones go around panhandling like professionals. One in ten *bomzhi* in Moscow is a child.

In what other country of the world would a state, in building a new life, sacrifice its own descendants?

---

* Russian acronymn for *bez opredelyonnogo mesta zhitelstva*, "without definite place of residence."—Trans.

Chapter 6

There's a Future, But Not for Us

The other day I had company. I ran out of cigarettes and decided to borrow some from my neighbor so I wouldn't have to go down to the store. My neighbor wasn't there, but her sixteen-year-old daughter, Tanya, was home preparing for entrance exams for an art school. She was studying to the point of exhaustion and hallucination.

"You know," she complained to me, "last night I thought I saw red roaches crawling up the wall. I went over and touched them and there was nothing there. But my father yelled at me and said, 'Don't you dare sleep. Keep drawing.' It's shameful if I, the daughter of an artist, can't get into the institute for the second year now. But what can I do if half the applicants get in through connections and the rest pay outrageous money for the slots with tuition? People like me are just swept aside. Even if you bend over backwards to pass, they'll find something to pick on, give you an F, and that's it."

Tanya was in the gloomiest of moods and terribly drained and hungry. "I'm so awfully lonely. Could I come over to your apartment?" she asked, and of course I said yes.

Tanya is a charming creature, slender, fragile, with bright clear eyes in a thin little face with prominent cheekbones. Even her funny, shapeless smock—Moscow's young people are wearing such things nowadays—and her thick-soled boots could not ruin her looks. They even gave her a kind of unique charm. She was almost like a refined lady out of a Turgenev novel, not like all the numerous other crude girls who grabbed whatever they wanted. She was touching, but far from a naive duckling.

Now Tanya had tears in her eyes; she was on the edge of hysteria. What was I to do with her? First, a tablet to calm her. Then a meal. A little glass of good sherry and a cup of strong coffee.

We ate and drank for a while, and I saw that she had relaxed and was warming up and becoming talkative. Once she got chatting you couldn't stop her. Mostly she talked about young people. Obviously she had a lot to get off her chest. And I wanted to listen. Thus our exchange mainly took the form of a monologue, with occasional leading questions sprinkled in by me.

GD: What is life like for young people now? What are the trends?

TANYA: Basically they listen to music. That's the extent of any trends, although I suppose you can divide young people into several categories.

First of all, there are the *majors*.* They live off their rich parents. Actually we all live off our parents, but these kids live very well. For the past two years I've been going to a major school where the girls have been wearing mink coats and diamonds since childhood. They drive to school in Mercedes with their pockets full of dollars. They even earn some good money themselves—their parents have gotten them into various dance ensembles so they're always going on tours abroad. They're just obsessed with their money. They think they can do anything. The majors set the tone in school and they're very smart talkers—sometimes you don't know what to say to them. Their favorite thing is to put somebody else down.

There are exceptions, of course. For example my girlfriend Vera wants to get into journalism school and has already published some articles. She's very smart. Her

* The term *majors* (*mazhory*) comes from a late 1980s song called "The Majors" by the rock group DDT:

> *Hats off to you, sons of diplomats,*
> *Ministers, lawyers, professors,*
> *Rich actresses, big journalists,*
> *Best-selling poets, and superstars.*
> *Everyone's calling for encores.*
> *You get in everywhere without a pass!*
>
> *Open your mouths, take off your hats,*
> *Down the street come the major brats!*
>
> *No-good trash.*
> *Do they have a soul? No? What do they care?*
> *How easy it is for these snot-nosed brats*
> *Daddy will find them a cushy job!*
> *Daddy will make everyone cheer,*
> *Daddy will cater to their every whim!*

father works with Yeltsin and her brother works for a foreign television station. Then there's Nina, an example of someone just the opposite. Her mother used to be a prostitute. Then she started going on shopping trips to Turkey and now she's in the rag trade. She's got a fairly large wholesale business now, so she isn't just traveling with suitcases. There were also some girls in that school whose mothers were being kept by rich lovers. In general, the majors' parents aren't very refined, they're small-time traders. I don't know whether I'm just unlucky and ended up in a group like that, or whether there are really an awful lot of them.

Another category are the gangsters (*bandity*). Sometimes they're also called *bulls*. They're involved in racketeering, mainly against their fellow classmates. They also stalk old ladies and sometimes kill them in order to take over their apartments. They draw up fake deeds, pay a notary public for a forged signature and stamp, and they're all set. Then they sell the apartment for huge bucks to the mafia. I know a gangster who lives in the building next door. He was kicked out of school after the seventh grade. He has so many cars that I've lost track of them. Actually he's really sweet to me. He thinks I'm a kid and takes care of me. You know, I can even rely on him.

Yeah, young people do not have much intellectual life. The majors at least have a superficial pretense of refinement—they can talk about books and the theater—but the bulls are zeroes. Nonentities. You know, they always wear leather jackets, sweat pants, and sneakers, like a uniform. But the mafia doesn't let them in on the big-time deals. They're just lookouts, errand boys.

The last year and a half I've gotten to like extreme

music. I go to the Arbat* often. There's an underpass there called the Pipe where my friend Zhorzhik goes busking. His music is terrible, but there's a very interesting crowd there. I'm especially intrigued by the *podonki* (scum). No, *podonok* isn't a swearword anymore, but more like a compliment. The *podonki* now include kids who like heavy metal music, called *metallisty*, the punks (*panky*), and in general people who are nonconformist in their thinking and lifestyles. I'm really attracted to these nonconformists. Actually the punks are dying out as a trend. They still hang out on the streets, but less and less. Basically these are boys fourteen to eighteen who just like to dress funny. No, they're not very dirty, but their clothes are all ripped to shreds. They wear dreadlocks—they wind colored threads into their hair to make little braids. See, they made me one! [Tanya proudly displayed her little braid.] They're funny. I wanted to become a punk, but then I saw that these people were just getting totally blasted all the time.

Then there are the hippies who walk barefoot down the Arbat. They're different now. The peace and love stuff is still there but they are much younger. They're total babies. And you know, sometimes you get the impression that they are mentally ill. But neither the punks nor the hippies nor anyone else have any real ideas in their heads. The Evil Empire has collapsed—now who do you fight? Now there are only the outward symbols.

GD: Where do they get money? What do they live on?

* A shopping arcade in the center of Moscow and also the name of the metro stop in the area. Entrances to Moscow subways are often connected to underpasses where street musicians, vendors, and beggars congregate.—TRANS.

TANYA: It depends. With the bulls and the majors, it's obvious—they all steal or get it from their parents. The punks have sticky fingers as well. There are the *gopniki** who are real toughs—terrible people. They can go up to a person and strip him right in broad daylight. They work in packs, like wolves. They don't stop at anything. As for the rest— some sell on the black market, or work parttime or their old man tosses them something to live on. . . .

GD: What schools are kids trying to get into now?

TANYA: The law schools are the most prestigious. Everything that's connected with money in the future is considered prestigious, especially advertising and making television commercials. For example, this year there was a huge flood of applications to the school of journalism (there's a new department there, training advertising specialists†). Many people want to become economists, financiers, managers— that is, to acquire knowledge that is in demand now in the private sector. Moscow State University is as prestigious as it was before. We call it the "faculty of aristocratic parents"— everything is through connections there. There's no competition at all to get into the trade schools or teachers' colleges. Actually young people don't feel like studying at all. Everyone only wants to make money, and shirk their studies. How do they earn money? Either they'll work after they

---

* Possibly from the Russian underworld slang *gopnat'*, to wander the streets and live as a vagrant.—TRANS.

† Under the Soviet system, "journalism" was unquestioningly combined with government propaganda, so perhaps it is not surprising that in the new commercial Russia advertising courses are not considered out of place in a journalism school.—TRANS.

graduate or look for some other way. Some have their parents find them a job, some trade in the commodities houses. Tougher kids go and work in security for various companies. Three hundred thousand rubles ($150) a month right out of school—that's not so bad.

GD: What universities are your classmates from the "major" school getting into?

TANYA: Five of them immediately went abroad. One of them even said, "Only poor people go to college. But I have rich parents. They have their own home in Germany." Some of them got into Moscow State University, mainly into the law school. You have to pay 20 million rubles ($10,000) for five years. By the way, you have to pay a million and a half rubles a year even at the art school that I want to go to, in the tuition-paid department. Every school sets its own fees. You can't figure them out. The most interesting thing is that this money doesn't go to the teachers but supposedly goes to remodeling the buildings, the dorms, and so on. So how come the quality of the buildings never improves? At the art schools now the most fashionable subject is commercial graphic design. But I have my own dream of becoming a set designer although it pays really badly. There are only thirty slots in the theater department and fifteen of them require tuition. The rest are through connections. So I realize that my chances are almost zero.

The rest of the kids just don't go to school. They go clubhopping.

GD: Tanya, what do young people do for fun?

TANYA: Nothing special. Nobody collects stamps or coins or anything anymore. Nobody especially gets into sports either—it's too expensive. They listen to music. Or else they do drugs a lot. They smoke *shmal*.

GD: What's *shmal?*

TANYA: Grass; half hashish and half poppy resin. Cocaine costs too much. Where do they get it? Oh, it's really easy. You go to Gogol Boulevard, for instance, and deaf mutes come up to you right away and start gesturing—do you want anything? A *boks* [matchbox] of *shmal* costs 30,000 rubles (about $15) and will make about four joints. All my friends smoke *shmal*.

GD: Why?

TANYA: Everybody has problems. They don't have the strength to endure them. It's an escape from reality. I sometimes break away from reality, too, but not that way—I read books or just take a walk down the street. Another thing people do is pills. There are lots of barbiturates. They say you get amazing hallucinations from them. Sniffing glue and huffing solvents is out, but LSD is hip. There are even acid clubs called "LSDance." It's terrible, drugs plus trance music, all with computers. It's hard to take even when you're not high. But a lot of people like it.

As soon as you walk into school you smell hash. You can't breathe. How do the teachers react? Normally. Once I saw this really young teacher standing on the stairs and a student was giving her a locomotive.

GD: What's that?!

TANYA: A locomotive is when you take a lighted *papiros** filled with *shmal* and blow the smoke through it into another person's mouth. I stood and watched for a long time—was I dreaming? They started having fines in our school: one thousand rubles (50 cents) for being tardy, 3,000 rubles ($1.50) for smoking cigarettes on school grounds, 5,000 rubles ($2.50) for making out, 7,000 ($3.50) for drinking booze, and 10,000 rubles ($5) for smoking hash on school grounds.

GD: It would be interesting to see your hangouts and your clubs.

TANYA: They're not interesting. Little boys of sixteen and seventeen with serious expressions playing at being grownups. Drugs, sex, and guns—mainly air pistols—and really serious fights. All the girls carry mace cans with them.

GD: What if you have to go out on the street at night alone? Do they catch you?

TANYA: The bulls would, without hesitation. But the *metallisty*, the *baykeri* (bikers), and *rokery* (rockers) don't touch you—just the opposite, they protect you. They have a code of honor. They really take care of girls. The majors just think of a girl as a bed accessory, but the others are very democratic in relationships between the sexes.

GD: Is there still such a thing as true love?

---

* A type of cheap Russian filterless cigarette with tobacco at one end and an empty paper holder at the other. The tobacco is replaced with grass.—TRANS.

TANYA: Sometimes, but not often. The girls just try to pump as much money as possible out of the boys. Especially blondes, the pretty ones.

GD: So what do kids do for fun?

TANYA: They go to the discos. The cheapest cost 10,000 rubles ($5) for girls and 20,000 rubles ($10) for boys. Others start at $25 a head and more. Where do kids get the money? From their parents. I know this girl Masha who gets $100 a week in pocket money from her parents. She goes to the *Bely tarakan* [White Roach]—that's a bar, a prestigious one—to sit for awhile, have a beer or a coffee. They have money from some shady deals. I have only one girlfriend whose family has financial difficulties. Her mother works at a radio station, and sits up all night doing translations. Really, I can't understand where people get money. Everybody has gone crazy over money now. They don't want to look to the future. It's money for the sake of money—it's disgusting. I'm lucky at least that among my friends there are people who think about the fate of Russia.

GD: So what *do* you young people think about the fate of Russia?

TANYA: A lot of them just throw up their hands. Few people believe things will get better. There have been a lot of suicides. It's fear, pessimism, and drugs. Thinking about the future is awful. Because there isn't one. Or actually there is one, but not for us somehow.

GD: Would you like to leave Russia?

TANYA: Yes and no. In Russia a person is not paid what he is worth at all. And we don't know the first thing about how to value ourselves. But it would be hard for me to adapt, and besides, my country is my world. I would probably be very homesick. I have to live here.

GD: What do you think about politics?

TANYA: No one could care less. It's all a dirty game. Before they used to feed you this ideological crap; now it's all about the economy. The people who were in the White House in October 1993 were either schizos or accidental passersby. It's true there are fanatics and real romantics, but that's not typical. In fact I can partly understand those fascists: when there's so much nastiness and filth around, you want to take a gun in your hand and cleanse everything.

We sat up late that night. I so wanted everything to work out for Tanya. But several days later I ran into her mother and found out that Tanya had not been accepted at art school. Once again. A bribe had been demanded—$3,000. Tanya's parents just didn't have that kind of money. Their connections also turned out to be insufficient. So apparently Tanya was right: "There's a future, but not for us."

∽

When I found out that there are special universities in Japan for the elderly, I experienced a real shock. Old folks who wish to make their life more interesting can study and do some socializing. Happy is the country whose older generation is not thrown on the scrap heap of history, I thought.

My parents spent their youth in the small provincial

Russian town of Tambov. Few of their classmates are still
alive—age, illness, and the stresses of recent years have taken
their toll. My mother's closest friend sends some news from
time to time. She can't travel to Moscow because it's too
expensive and her health wouldn't allow it anyway. A telephone call is also too costly. So letters are the last thread of
connection—and they sometimes get lost in the mail. Each
letter is a *cri de coeur*, leaving a bitter aftertaste in the soul.

First Letter
Dear Viktoria,
    I haven't written you in a long time and haven't
had any news from you. Life is such now that there's
no certainty in it. I hope you get my letter.
    I have been sick for half a year now. It's shame-
ful to complain at my age but you know how it is. In
June I landed in the hospital (I fainted on the street and
suffered skull and brain injury as a result). The head-
aches torment me and my heart is acting up. I'm living
on medications and shots. The ambulance comes to my
house two or three times a month.
    My life is cheerless. My monthly pension is
21,000 rubles—about $14. [Pensions for the elderly have
been raised recently, but the additional amount is not
significant.] That's what I've gotten from the state for
losing my health—now I'm a second-group disabled
person.* That's my reward for faithful service for thirty-
seven years. Yura and Nadya, my cousins who live in

* Under the Soviet system (retained by the Russian government), disabled persons
are divided into groups according to the severity of their disability, with a corresponding scale of pensions.—TRANS.

Volgograd, help me out. They're relatives, but it's still a handout. It's shameful that I've lived to such an age and I'm not capable of taking care of myself. They call our generation the "red-browns"* now, almost fascists; they say we have ruined life for the young people, but in fact they're now selling off what we made with our own hands. Perhaps I've gone crazy from old age and don't understand anything?

I've left my cousins my privatized apartment in my will so that the swindlers don't get my apartment after my death.

The market has everything—but at what prices? There's a lot of meat, which seems to be a good thing, but in reality they're butchering the cattle because it's not profitable to keep them. What will come next? Not only will there be no meat but no milk or butter. What will happen to us? It's all in God's hands.

Yours,

Mariya

Second Letter

Dear Viktoria,

I got your news and am writing back right away. Otherwise it might be too late because it seems my life is coming to an end.

It's sickening to look at those self-satisfied, well-fed mugs on the television screen discussing the fate of Russia, while they themselves are recklessly stealing it

---

* Red for Communists and brown for fascists. Die-hard Communists who have switched to Russian nationalist causes are branded "red-browns."—Trans.

and selling it off. All we can do is quietly and silently die because whether we shout or not, no one will hear our voices. Recently I read about the tragic case of Yumatov, that famous actor of our generation. He got drunk, went outside, got into a ridiculous quarrel over some dog, and shot a man with a hunting rifle. When they came to arrest him, they found he had nothing in his house—not a television, no furniture, almost bare walls. That's the level of poverty he'd sunk to! Yet he had been famous in our day, had played the parts of war heroes and model workers. It just doesn't make sense. He probably took to the bottle from bitterness and disappointment. I can imagine what his poor wife went through.

I already wrote you that I'm living on medications. But I do want to live. My doctor tries to calm me, telling me it will all pass, but I realize that he's just placating me.

Can you imagine, I was forced to appeal to the social services for help! It's shameful, but what can you do? After all, I *can't* just keep bothering the neighbors all the time. So now they're delivering bread, milk, and medications to me.

As you know, I don't have any relatives in the city. When I feel bad I call the ambulance, crawl my way to the door, open it, and lie down on the floor. Then the doctors pick me up themselves. I've gotten to know some of them because they have come a number of times.

Who would ever have imagined that our old age would be like this? A lot of our cohorts have already passed into the next world.

I've been thinking of you along these lines: Do you go to church? Have you resolved such a difficult question for yourself—do you believe in God or not? I'm sorry, I know that this question is sensitive and delicate but in our society many shortcomings are due precisely to a lack of faith in God.

When I am in church, and that's none too often since I don't have the strength to get there, I cry when I hear how they are praying for our country and for our soldiers. I'm really sick of constantly thinking about getting food and talking about money. I am a pessimist and I think that we can't expect anything. Even from the younger generation, for that matter. I'm sick of all this foreign stuff, too, to the point of nausea. They talk about a renaissance of Russia, but the real Russian people, the Russian Orthodox, are perishing.

I simply can't comprehend the degree of savagery now in Russia! I wrote you that I left Yura and Nadya my privatized apartment in my will. So, imagine, these shady characters came to visit me and offered to buy it for a song. They were out-and-out gangsters. They were hinting that if I didn't go along with them nicely, they'd get a hold of my apartment anyway. And really, they said, you're such an ancient old bag, anything could happen. You could fall on the street or drown in your bathtub or take the wrong medication. They were threatening me, you see. I called the police but they wouldn't move a muscle. I have a bad heart. I walk around afraid now. Well, what of it? Our town is small, apartments aren't as valuable as they are for you in Moscow. I was reading in the newspapers what's going on in Moscow; it sends chills up my spine. They write that it's open season on old folks because of apartments. Is that true? In the old days people used to poison each other with mercury over living space but now they torture and murder people and cut the corpses up into bits and throw them in the garbage. Anything to get a hold of an apartment and then sell it to some rich man. Young people are paving the road for themselves over the dead bodies of old folks. Nobody needs us and we just irritate everyone with the way that we just won't die and free up a place for them. There are even some children who deliberately put their elderly parents in the loony bin so they won't be in the way—and once the old folks get near the genuine crazy people they go out of their minds for real, from despair and sorrow at their children's treachery. I don't have any children, so God spared me that at least.

Now they even register so-called marriages with dead people. A certain operator learned that an old lady had died and ran to a notary public at city hall. For a bribe he got them to put a later date on the death certificate, so now this brand-new "widower" becomes the sole owner of the apartment and all her possessions.

So take care of yourself.

Yours,
Mariya

Third Letter
Hello Viktoria,

I'm sick of writing about my illnesses, so I won't bother you with them anymore. But I so want to have a heart-to-heart talk with a person close to me. I often recall our student years. It was a great time—after the war, with hunger, but somehow bright and joyful. It seemed as if everything would be good and life would go on as it should. But no, it didn't turn out like that. It was a brutal mistake. Life never belonged to us—not then, not now. Do you remember what Lermontov* wrote?

> *Farewell, unwashed Russia,*
> *Country of slaves, country of masters,*
> *And you, blue uniforms,*
> *And you, people loyal to them.*

I taught Russian literature all my life in school and tried to raise children to respect their own people, and now I realize that I myself can't respect and love a people who make a mockery of themselves, who degrade themselves so. Essentially nothing has changed in Russia since the time of Lermontov. True, the masters and the color of the uniforms have changed, but the slaves have remained just the same. All of us are slaves. I don't know what made us this way. I'm not a historian and it's not mine to judge such peculiarities of the Russian psychology as lackeydom and a slavish character. But it's a fact. Happy is he who has squeezed out the slave in himself drop by drop. But almost all the people like that died in Stalin's labor camps. Now slavery is rooted in our genes.

I have the right to say these bitter things be-

---

* Mikhail Lermontov, the popular nineteenth-century Russian poet and novelist.—TRANS.

cause I myself committed a slavish act at one time. I rejected my beloved for the sake of the Party. Remember when I was sent to Yakutia on assignment after the institute, to a rural school?* Nearby was a settlement of political exiles. I met a man there and fell in love with him. He was from the Baltic, much older than me, and had wound up in exile for hating the Soviet government. I was called into the authorities and told, either forget him, or give up your Party card. So I buckled. How many times I chastised myself for that! After all, he was my first and last love. I never married, never had children, and now I'm all alone. But sometimes I selfishly think that perhaps it's a good thing. There's no one to yearn over. Look how many unhappy families were scattered all over the place after the collapse of the Union! A ticket from Magadan to Moscow costs $1,000 —is it really conceivable to find money like that for a poor old lady who wants to visit her grandson?

A society of social justice—how immoral, how cynical that sounds! Our state took away the surplus product† from us all our lives, robbed us, exploited us like slaves—and is now forcing young people to give back to us part of our earnings through the social secu-

---

* Yakutia is a northern region of Siberia. Under the Soviet system, after graduation from higher education, students were assigned by the state to jobs throughout the country. Those with better grades and connections got the plusher jobs in Moscow or other urban centers; most were sent to places far from their homes. The three-year assignment provided both job training and a way to repay the state for education.—TRANS.

† A Marxist term signifying the amount a worker produces above and beyond his due wages and expenses. The capitalists were said to exploit workers and confiscate this excess.—TRANS.

rity pension fund. We're hanging around young people's necks. What reason do they have to love us? Why such humiliation? Where is the money that we earned? Who has used it to build villas and dachas for themselves?

I heard that there are new pension funds through which one can invest money ahead of time to provide security for old age. But I don't have that kind of money—and then I don't believe in it—in our country of thieves and swindlers, any noble undertaking turns to fraud.

My God, where are we headed? I lie here alone the whole day and keep thinking and thinking. What did Russia do to deserve such a fate, such torment? We are dying out—both physically and mentally. We are becoming degraded—both morally and genetically. God help Russia!

Forgive me for writing such a letter. It will seem a little emotional to you, but I wanted to share my worries with someone. I feel so bad that I'm afraid that this letter is one of the last.

Yours,
Mariya

After this one, no more letters came from Mariya, and no one answers the telephone in her apartment.

❧

Sometimes I take a tape recorder, camera, and, just in case, a can of mace and head out to wander the streets of Moscow in search of something interesting. Sometimes I take Dasha with me. She loves these adventures and calls them

"going on an expedition." These jaunts serve several pur-
poses at once for me. First, I want to awaken in my daughter
an interest in journalism and information in general. Second,
I want to show her, since she's really a spoiled little girl, how
badly some people live and that since nothing is going to fall
from the sky on its own, you have to earn it. Third, when
you have such a trusting creature along with you with such
wide-open eyes, people are more likely to talk to you.

That day I was gathering material on a special category of old people—those rejected by society. I didn't have
to go far—their gathering places are well known and include
the metro stations, churches, train stations, and the underground passages.

No sooner did I walk into the metro than I encoun-
tered a tragedy: a middle-aged woman with two babies in a
carriage was standing with a sign that read Their Parents
Were Killed. Please Help. Nearby sat an old disabled man
with a cap in front of him containing coins, and next to
him—separately—some rose-colored legs cut off at the knee.
Artificial limbs, I realized belatedly, but still the scene was
so surreal that I was shaken.

Two beggars got on the train. They stunk so badly
that everybody quickly backed away to the other end of the
car. One of them had deliberately torn his pants to reveal a
terrible ulcer—a phony one, it seemed to me. In the passageway at the metro exit stood a refugee woman from Armenia, and lying right on the cement in front of her was a
fairly big boy about eight years old. In another passage an
ugly old woman was collecting alms. On the whole the scene
was a strong brew of sorrow and fraud, poverty and greed,
suffering and lies, so that it was impossible to tell what was
true and what was false.

Still I decided to talk to some of the characters that seemed particularly interesting to me. At the entrance to a church sat an old lady with the ancient, wrinkled face of an icon, who seemed to be at least a hundred years old. She was not even begging for alms—the little box in front of her was empty—she was just sitting and watching the people passing by, like in the theater. Her gaze was aged and apathetic. I struck up a conversation with her. Oddly enough she replied rather enthusiastically, although each word seemed to take thirty seconds to fall from her mouth.

She was born in 1914. She lived alone in a communal apartment. She had a son, but he didn't visit her, although he did pay for her room quite punctually. Her monthly pension was 20,000 rubles ($10), but was enough to live on.

"How could that be enough?" I asked in surprise. "What do you eat?"

"I go to the *pelmennaya*,* my child," the old lady explained. "I eat what the customers leave on their plates. People don't give much change here, some days not even a kopeck, but I still keep coming. It's so awfully boring to sit at home. When you come here it's more cheery. It's like you're seeing the world a little."

"Did you vote in the elections?"

The woman unexpectedly grew animated.

"Of course I did."

"Who did you vote for?"

"I don't know."

"Well, do you even recall a name?"

"I don't remember anything. My head aches."

---

* Cheap fast-food restaurant selling *pelmeni*, a meat or vegetable patty similar to ravioli.—TRANS.

"Who do you like more, Yeltsin or Zhirinovsky?"

"Well, I don't know. Yeltsin, I suppose."

"Who do you want to be the new president?"

"I don't want anybody."

"What do you think about the shelling of the White House?"

The old lady was silent for a long time, apparently trying to remember what this White House was. Then she suddenly blurted, "I think that I wish that my death would come sooner!" and fell silent.

Realizing that there was no point in hanging around, we crossed over to the street vendors. At first they turned away, but when they saw Dasha they softened and began to answer questions.

One was a former bookkeeper, now sixty years old. Even so, her pension was the same as that of the other old lady who had been a cleaning woman. Street-vending didn't bring in much of an income—a maximum of 2,000 to 3,000 rubles a day, and that was only if the police or the racketeers didn't take it away. So the main thing wasn't the money, I surmised. This was about a lack of attention from society, about loneliness.

This woman didn't like the democrats or the conservatives. She just couldn't see any difference between them. Before she used to respect Yeltsin, but now she didn't trust him.

"What about Zhirinovsky?"

"I think he's not a bad person," she said somewhat cautiously. "The pensioners will have it good with him."

Dasha listened to all this with her mouth open.

"Mama," she said later. "How can it be? Grownup people, and they don't get the difference between Yeltsin and

Zhirinovsky! And really, how do they live? Nobody needs them!"

"You see, daughter," I replied. "The second point is worse than the first. Other people will come to take Yeltsin's and Zhirinovsky's place, but these old ladies will remain the same as they always were—nobody needs them at all. That's the real tragedy."

When I later looked at the photographs I had taken during such expeditions, I noticed something strange. The satisfied, well-fed old men, the strong young fellows, the sprightly teenagers, came out right—vivid and in focus. But the images of the pathetic and even hideous inevitably came out smudged and blurry somehow. At first I blamed my camera and even decided to buy a new one, until an acquaintance explained to me with a smile, "The problem isn't your camera, but you. When you take pictures of normal people, your hand doesn't tremble. But when you try to snap the cripples and the beggars as quickly as possible so they aren't offended, the camera shakes."

Our last expedition was particularly unpleasant. I was writing an article on the homeless. As soon as we boarded the metro car, I was lucky enough to find a "live subject." There on the seat was an amazing tramp such as I have never seen even in the movies. He was horrendously filthy, ragged, and smelly. Something was moving in his tangled hair. He had a terrible sore on his nose. He was sleeping like a baby, his mouth open, dreaming. The city was his home, and the metro was his bedroom. Even standing near him was unpleasant, but the smartly dressed women sitting next to him were not repulsed.

I took out my camera and snapped a picture. The passengers gave me angry sideward glances, but kept silent. When the flashbulb went off a second time, the public couldn't restrain themselves. A flood of choice swearwords poured down upon me. People threatened to "punch me in the mug," break my camera, and take me to the police. Me—and not that antisocial homeless man! If this had happened a few years ago, I would have been grabbed and taken down to the KGB for sure—which once did happen to me on Kalinin Avenue when I was working at the radio station and in complete innocence interviewing someone about the upcoming New Year's holiday. Now I realized that no amount of perestroika and glasnost could change the mentality of the masses: a beggar, a filthy parasite will evoke more sympathy in people than a member of the intelligentsia with a camera. My crime was that I had tried to bring the hidden out into the open. And in general people have always pitied the beggars in old Russia. Perhaps because compared to a beggar, one doesn't seem so pathetic oneself.

While I was arguing with the public, several more equally colorful characters passed through the car. All were supposedly refugees, and all had children with them—children with puffy, ashen faces, asleep in adults' arms. The adults demanded money from the passengers in well-modulated voices. Really, in my view, the first reaction of a policeman upon seeing such a child should be to take the "refugee" down to the precinct to check if the child had been kidnapped. After all, kids are stolen right out of their strollers in stores!

But no, none of this concerned anybody. There are up to a hundred thousand vagrants in Moscow and about half a million throughout the whole former Soviet Union. If you add to that the illegal refugees from Southeast Asia, Central Asia, and Africa, the number is impressive. The vagrants love Moscow the most; it's a rich city.

How do they become homeless? In different ways.

Some drink up their rent money—or their apartment itself, when they sell it off. Others come here after getting out of prison, in order to get rich, but find the competition too fierce. Still others are thrown out on the street by their own children.

I was particularly shocked by a story I read in the paper about young women who come here from other republics to give birth to children and beg. After they collect enough money, they abandon the children and disappear.

One of the beggars admitted that she collected up to 8,000 rubles ($4) by going through the metro cars several times. After I counted how many cars she could cover a day without too much of a strain, I reached a figure that was many times more than the highest monthly salary of a Moscow University professor.

The homeless fight a terrible battle for survival among themselves, and the weak are doomed to defeat. The weakest are pushed into an underground city—they live among the hot-water pipes, and because of frequent accidents they are sometimes boiled alive. Mostly the homeless live at the train stations or in abandoned buildings.

I gazed at the photographs for a long time—at faces in which nothing human remained—and I wondered what was to blame for this. The depravity of human nature? The evil whim of fate? The indifference of the government? Probably each of these answers is partly true, but that doesn't make it any easier. Understanding the problem does not alleviate the problem itself. Thus the beggars and the homeless wander the Russian looking-glass world like kings, spreading infection and swelling the ranks of the criminals. And that is also a sign of our reality, because only in an upside-down society do the beggars sometimes live a more satiated and privileged life than decent, upright citizens.

Chapter 7

Sovs, Hacks, and Freeloaders

What can I say about Russia? It's all scamming, ripping off, and freeloading.

—the diary of Dasha Dutkina, age 10

Much has been written about Russia, this "mystery wrapped in an enigma." Oh, the inscrutable profundity of the Russian East, this fusion of Europe and Asia, so fascinating to the philosophers and writers! Many have tried to unravel the mystery hidden in the soul of Russia. But it is only at first glance that Russia is unique, great, and unified. In reality there are many Russias, like fantastic parallel universes. The fate of a specific individual depends solely upon which of these Russias he has been destined to inhabit, whether the country of harsh submission or the country of unlimited freedom of spirit; the country of angelic holiness or of beastly profanity; in the Russia of geniuses, or of the faceless masses. Perhaps some will find such a cocktail of philosophy and science fiction strange, but isn't this monstrous brew in itself peculiar, this blend of such terribly contradictory features in one nation? For even after solving the riddle concealed within the soul of Russia, we still come up against a brick wall. How could such a strange creature arise—like the mythological Chinese *qilin*—with the body of a deer, the horn of a unicorn, the neck of a wolf, the tail of a bull, and the hooves of a horse?

The Russia of genius, the Russia of angelic holiness and unlimited freedom of spirit, is known to quite a few, thanks to Russian classical literature, art, music, philosophy, and science—and thanks to Russian patriotism and readiness for self-sacrifice. The world has heard enough about the brutal baseness of the Russians as well—starting with the bloody history of the Middle Ages and ending with the tragic fates of the White emigrés and the prisoners of the Stalin era.

Let us talk rather about what has always remained off-camera somehow—the faceless masses. Those same masses that in Russian are abstractly called *narod*, the people, the folk. Those very masses that make up the major portion of the nation—and in the final analysis decide in elections who will take the helm of power in Russia. Among the fantastic parallel worlds of Russia, this is one that is all too real.

∾

There is a secret thread upon which the beads of the endless Russian contradictions can easily be strung. That thread is our national psychology. All of us are Russians— a government official, a ballerina, an academician, a street-sweeping bum—because in certain circumstances the same coiled springs of the Russian character can be released. The religious philosopher Nikolai Berdyayev came the closest of anyone to this secret. Not only was he able to unravel the mystery of the Russian soul, he was able to place the contents of this soul on shelves and in boxes, meticulously sticking the right labels upon them. Now whoever wishes to understand, predict, and rule has only to take the box needed from the right shelf and apply its contents to the given situation, merely making a few modifications for modern times. After all, quite a lot of water has gone under the bridge since the turn of this century when Berdyayev wrote. And much that is new has appeared in our soul under the press of circumstance.

Long ago, an ice age killed off the dinosaurs but other carnivores and herbivores who were more nimble and adaptable to the new conditions flourished. Likewise, the thawing of the cold war era saw the end of *homo Sovieticus*. In the time since, what sort of beasts have emerged in Russia in place of the old dinosaurs? And who are these reptiles who have multiplied now under the tender sun of "freedom" granted by perestroika and reform?

We all have lived for so many years in proximity to the zone—and some right in it—that now it turns out that practically the whole country speaks the slang of prisons, labor camps, and criminals. Many of these words, like other coarse language, sully the formerly great and pure Russian language, and are alternately humorous and horrifying. Sometimes the uninitiated cannot guess the secret, hidden meaning in familiar-sounding words, but like the three wheels, the three pillars, or the three cornerstones upon which rests the world, there are three all-encompassing words upon which the universe of the post-Soviet psychology is upheld: *sovok*, *khaltura*, and *khalyava*. Unlike *sputnik* or *glasnost*, these Russian terms are not known to the foreign reader, and even a specialist in Russian culture would most likely find it difficult to explain them completely. Nevertheless, these three words define with greatest accuracy the psychology of the post-Soviet citizen and the moral climate in Russia today.

The slang of the prisons, labor camps, and underworld of the Stalinist zone defined the word *sovok*, or *sov*, in two ways. First, as *Sovetskaya vlast*, Soviet power or government, and secondly as *Sovetskiy Soyuz*, the Soviet Union. (The very sound of the word conveys a pejorative nuance because its homonym means "scoop" or "dustpan," a thing used to pick up garbage.) Now *sovok* is defined differently. A sov is generally a person raised in the traditions of socialist egalitarian ideology, with all the resultant personality traits (including a slavish attitude toward authority). In other words, *homo Sovieticus* was a sov. Strictly speaking, all of us—and perhaps even our children—are to some extent still sovs, but a classic, 100-percent sov stands out immediately. Still a sov is not necessarily a worker or peasant. A sov can just as easily be (or not be) someone in any profession or social group, from a janitor to a professor, from a writer to a pig tender, from the faceless masses to the ruling elite.

The habit of slavery was programmed into the Russian character from the time of the Mongolian-Tatar Yoke, and was reinforced in the years of cheerless serfdom. Normally a slave will work only under the fear of reprisal. As soon as the reins are slackened even a little bit, he tries to shirk his job and crawl off to the side. Thus we came to know the charms of Andropov's campaign for labor discipline in the 1980s. Any policeman or auxiliary had the full right to demand to see the identification of people sitting in cafes, restaurants, or movie theaters or even just walking down the street, and to expect an explanation for why they were not at their jobs in the middle of the workday. Official reports to places of employment were written against "violators" who were unable to come up with convincing reasons; sometimes this even led to their dismissal. Then Gorbachev's perestroika and the reforms of Yegor Gaidar and Anatoly

Chubais* opened up untold prospects for the aggressively indolent. They bestowed those sov loafers with ample opportunities for hackwork and freeloading.

Nowadays—thanks to the reform!—lazy and irresponsible sovs no longer have to tremble with fear when they skip work. Work-shirkers have no reason to be afraid that they will be kicked out of Moscow under the criminal-code article penalizing "malicious parasitism," or failure to hold a job. Because now work is no longer obligatory, and in order to live well you don't even have to steal and murder. Why go to such extremes when there are such wonderful methods available as hackwork and freeloading! Now it is legalized and approved on a national scale. Have fun, people!

Khaltura is defined as "work on the side for extra earnings" and also (more accurately) "careless work performed haphazardly, hastily." *Khalyava* is defined as "receiving something for nothing, for free."

I have written about "working" on the side in some detail in previous chapters. But freeloading as an aspect of the Russian mentality, as a mirror of Russian life, is worthy of special discussion. Now I ask you, where but Russia would you find so many inspired freeloaders in the national folklore?

Take the typical Russian fairy tale in which an unwashed, uncombed, loafing bum named Ivan the Fool sits on top of a big stove of the sort that typically used to grace Russian homes. He is too lazy even to climb down to the floor, whereas his elder brothers labor by the sweat of their brows, earning a good living. Suddenly Ivan jumps off the

---

* Anatoly Chubais, former minister of privatization, now first deputy prime minister.—TRANS.

stove and scurries out of the cabin to catch a magic fish who will grant him three wishes. Or a magic horse named Sivkaburka appears, and Ivan blows in its ear, and spits three times and—presto, change-o—he has beat everyone, turned himself into a handsome rich man, and even won the tsar's daughter and half the tsardom to boot!

In the more than half a century of socialist egalitarianism, with a free crust of bread guaranteed to everyone, and with free (although poor) health care, housing, and public education, the habit of parasitism has irreversibly corrupted the Russian people. Thus millions of Russian television viewers have found endless Mexican soap operas to their taste, where the heroes, wilting under the blows of cruel fate for the whole series, are inevitably brought fortune in the end. The popularity of these shows has not only surpassed all Soviet and Western film masterpieces, literary scenarios following the formula of these sagas have become more cherished by the ordinary Russian than even the works of Pushkin, Lermontov, Gogol, Tolstoy, and Chekhov taken together—I won't even mention Dostoyevsky, who requires particular mental and emotional effort to read. These seeds from across the ocean fell on fertile ground and yielded abundant fruits—they bred new Ivan the Fool types by the millions, who dream of their own personal Firebird of Fortune.

When he began his privatization games, Anatoly Chubais solemnly vowed to create a class of property owners in Russia. Later, however, he renounced his promise, just as Peter denied Christ. It turned out, as he said, that "we had never set ourselves the task of making each citizen a property owner; the chief task of privatization was to provide each person with the opportunity to become a property owner!"[9]

An invisible sleight of hand (or tongue)—and the rabbit disappears from the hat.

After taking away their entire life's savings in a day, the state solemnly awarded each citizen a slip of paper called a voucher, which symbolized his or her portion of the national product. At the time the little piece of paper was worth 10,000 rubles. Now it's worth a little more, but even so, when converted to dollars, it is humiliatingly, ridiculously tiny—less than $5. A logical question arises: Who arrogated to themselves all these odd portions of the national wealth that supposedly belonged to a nonexistent class of property owners? Who, for example, decided that Beryozka, the Moscow store, is valued more than the entire Far Eastern fleet? Psychologically, the result of all these childish games with scraps of paper, investment funds, and ridiculous dividends is terrifying. Instead of the declared class of property owners who were to become the bulwark of a civilized state, Russia has got a rather well-established class of freeloaders.

Let us take a look at the television screen glowing in virtually every home. There's an irritating series of commercials that keeps flickering on the screen, interrupting the movies and the interesting shows for ten to fifteen minutes at a time. The leitmotif is unchanging: how to make big money. For nothing.

First commercial:
A withered little man of an indeterminate age appears on the screen. He takes a seat with a pompous expression. Before him is a spread of abundant opulence, like

the magic tablecloth of the Russian fairy tale that sets itself: wines, candies, imported pastries, caviar, champagne, fruits, coffee, and tea. You cannot take it all in during the span of the commercial, although it is obvious that the items represent affluence.

The little man, puffed up with pride, utters the following monologue: "You ask, what is a *rentier*? An investor— that's me. I don't work, my money's working for me. So-o-o?" he poses the question and gestures toward the magic table-cloth as if to say, see for yourselves.

The commercial was too abstract. It was not even clear who produced it and for whom it was intended, which is why it was soon removed from the air—but it performed its role. It capitalized on a great idea in the minds of the man on the street: the thought of how wonderful it is to live for free. Without lifting a finger.

The next commercials are far more specific and tar-geted at a very definite segment of the population. Their producers are soul-catchers—they are joint stock companies, trusts, commercial banks, and other financial institutions. Some of them film entire rags-to-riches sagas in the manner of the story of Lyonya Golubkov. All of them promise untold wealth—immediately, and for nothing.

Second commercial:
This time the television screen shows the obnoxious bearded face of a redhaired fellow who looks like the typical Slavophile.* The fellow is drinking tea and munching an

---

* In the nineteenth century the Slavophiles debated the Westernizers over Russia's future, advocating a uniquely Russian path of development and eschewing per-nicious Western influence. Slavophiles today can range from patriots to chauvin-istic nationalists.—TRANS.

enormous hero sandwich spread with red caviar. The man has invested his money in stock in the Doka-Bread Company and is now prospering. "There's enough for bread," he mumbles happily, and the translucent grains of caviar, bright red in the spotlights, fall from the gigantic sandwich and stick in his red, bushy beard.

Third commercial:

Two members of the intelligentsia, a father and son trying to look like intellectuals, are sitting on a bank fishing in the pouring rain. The son suddenly says dreamily, *"That's the way to do it!"* "What?" the father asks, puzzled. "Why, don't you see?" the son says in surprise. "We're sitting here and our money's working for us!" Then both of them drop their fishing rods and begin punching the buttons on their calculators like crazy men. This is a commercial for the Telemarket Company, which is supposedly investing in the creation of an integrated Russian communications system, but actually is bilking the public out of their money.

Of course these numerous financial companies and the dozens—hundreds—of other such fraudulent operations have no government license for such activity. Just like their investors, they have something else—a relentless, passionate desire to get rich quickly and easily.

Most likely some of the commercial producers realize, after all, how amoral they and their investors might appear, because sometimes "justifying" dialogue like this comes along:

"You're an idler, Lyonya, a freeloader," says the worker Ivan, the brother of Lyonya Golubkov. "I've been breaking my back for my whole life and never have earned anything and here you are raking in money for nothing. You freeloader!"

"I'm not a freeloader, I'm a partner," says Lyonya indignantly.

In the next commercial in the series both brothers are already traveling together to the world soccer championship in America—from which it follows that after racking his brains, brother Ivan finally realized that being a "partner" was easier and simpler than being an honest working stiff. The television viewer, already green with envy, is then finished off: The two brothers are shown dancing with Victoria Ruffo, the Mexican star who plays the main character in the extremely popular soap opera *Simply Maria*. "Maria" flashes an artificial smile and, like a windup doll, keeps giving the same answer to all questions: "Si, si!" But the viewer is in ecstasy at the sight. Indeed, among all the commercials, first prize unquestioningly goes to the MMM Joint Stock Company and its creation—"the mirror of Russian reform"—the half-prole, half-bum, but now prospering investor, Lyonya Golubkov.

In developed countries a person who has a lot of money becomes an investor, but in Russia it's all backward. Those who don't have any money at all dream of becoming investors. And no wonder! Because sweet-talking Alisa the Fox and Bazilio the Cat promise as much as a 1,600 percent annual return. The interest is automatically compounded on the principle, much to the envy of the rest of the world, where a 6 percent annual yield is an almost incredible figure.

There is a boom in private investment in Russia now. Millions of "partners" are investing their pennies (and sometimes quite respectable sums) in stocks, certificates of deposit, foreign currency, and other securities, dreaming of becoming millionaires within a few months. Not only is honest labor no longer respected; working fair and square has somehow become shameful and stupid. Poverty corrupts no less than wealth, especially if it turns into a dream of freeloading where sponging becomes the only panacea.

But are we worse off than we were before in the days before perestroika? After all, in the old days the ordinary citizen didn't exactly eat sandwiches with red caviar every day and drink imported beer. But the essence of the tragedy of the ordinary consumer can be expressed in one sentence: we are not just suffering inflation, but a radical alteration of the price structure. The darned thing about it is that in this chaos it is very hard for us to adapt and to figure out where we stand. I will cite a concrete example from my personal life.

After graduating from Moscow State University, my husband and I became young specialists, as they were called (something like trainees)—I as an editor at Moscow Radio and he as a consultant at the All-Union Copyright Agency (VAAP), both with knowledge of Japanese and English, with degrees in history. Together we earned 240 rubles per month. Even with our parents paying for the apartment, giving us clothing, buying furniture, and kicking in money and groceries, we did not have enough to live on. At the end of each month we regularly bummed 20 or 30 rubles from our friends and acquaintances and returned the debt on payday on the first of the following month. After five years we had "grown up" to earning a total of 400 rubles a month, plus my honoraria for articles and literary translations, so that within a year without particular strain we could save up for a used car.

Workers, especially skilled ones, earned a fairly decent wage. Engineers of various types and junior scientific researchers in academic institutions lived far more modestly, but as far as I recall even they did not groan as much as they do now. University professors, on the other hand, and government ministers received 500 to 600 rubles per month, and enjoyed an entirely comfortable, almost luxurious social life, taking off on foreign trips every year and inviting a full house of guests to their homes every week. Their housing was practically free, along with health care and education— the quality wasn't important. And I am not even mentioning the nomenklatura, who had long since been living solidly "under Communism."

Now the pyramid has been turned upside down, and those who were on top suddenly find themselves on the bottom. Students who never graduated from college, working part-time in commercial firms, get up to $200 a month for "petty expenses" (almost double the country's average wages). Meanwhile their parents, employed at state-subsidized organizations, do not collect their wages for months at a time due to the cash shortage. Even when they finally do get their pay, it is so small that they sometimes don't even manage to bring it home—they spend it all on the way. Yesterday's proud professors go around in torn jackets humbly begging for grants from foreign universities, whereas the blockheads who were expelled for academic failure five years ago are now the geniuses of the political and financial world. Yesterday's scam artists are now the cream of society, and yesterday's cream has gone sour and become the stinking dregs of society. Only the nomenklatura—both the old and the new—have hung on to their interests.

On the whole, it is difficult to compare the current situation with the old days; still, one small but substantial nuance reveals the essence of the change. For decades the state took our "surplus product," so of course most Russians were never rich. But through persistent, slavish labor people still somehow managed to put away some savings for their retirement—and for death, for a coffin and a set of fine clothes in which to be laid out. We were not rich then, but everything, especially food, was cheaper. By economizing on food, even families with very modest means could allow themselves to buy a set of furniture (sometimes two or three), certainly a television, a refrigerator, a washing machine, and a vacuum cleaner. Almost the entire middle class and a good share of the skilled workers had dachas (with their accompanying free plots of earth, which were distributed at the place of employment) and cars. People were able to acquire all these things because they cost almost next to nothing by world standards. Nobody was concerned about how these low prices were achieved—by selling off natural resources such as timber. The government feared popular discontent and tried to maintain the low prices and required selection of goods in stores until the very last moment, when the mechanism of the economy finally sprung loose.

Those were the days of universal freeloading, a government of handouts. Therefore, relatively poor as they were, people grew accustomed during the years of Soviet rule to not noticing their poverty, and were kept in an illusion of relative prosperity. Now people have had to part with all those cherished illusions along with their habit of hanging on the government's neck (because the state raised them, fed them, educated them, provided them with shoes and clothing—and did not leave them without work!). The state—that very same caring state—not only rudely and roughly awoke people from their sweet dreams, it in fact robbed them with the liberalization of prices and endless monetary reforms. It took away their savings, their relative prosperity, their vacations, and their confidence in the future.

We go to bed at night and wake up every morning with one unpleasant thought: What will become of us tomorrow if . . . This "if" has countless possible variations, each more horrible than the next.

But for now we thoughtlessly spend all our money (since it's useless to save it) on food and pretty rags, like feasting during the plague. Meanwhile the old necessities in our apartments are aging, rusting, or disintegrating. It is unthinkable now to buy new furniture, a television, refrigerator, or vacuum cleaner. Our rundown, ancient automobiles have to last out the century. What will be left when all of these finally die? Will our walls be bare? And what will become of a person who dies within those bare walls, without even enough savings for a funeral? A polyethylene bag and a spot in a common grave?

Admittedly we have always been relatively poor in the material sense but now we have been pushed into a poverty of spirit. After my friend's husband died of cancer her son entered the medical institute, solemnly vowing that he would save people from such a torturous death. He graduated with honors, interned for a year in England, and received wonderful commendations. Eight years passed. The salaries of doctors fell to among the lowest in society. Thus our genius doctor, after spending a year living off the salary of his wife who worked in a commercial firm, took up buying and reselling children's clothing.

Another of my acquaintances, a former designer, rented a little store and spent the summer selling vegetables. In the end he was barely able to cover his rent, and racketeers who quickly appeared on the scene threatened to take away even this amount. Thus the failed merchant dropped everything in a panic and has been hiding out for several months in a friend's apartment.

A neighbor of mine, a professional artist (and quite a good one) who had exhibited her works at international shows, no longer paints. She is occupied with far more important business now: having invested all her earnings in stocks, she now spends weeks standing in lines to collect her dividends in time.

Who are these people—a new lumpen or simply freeloaders? It is not an easy question. Some people dig garden beds and grow berries and vegetables to sell. Others stand outside the metro or in the passageways and outside stores selling cigarettes, salami, and vodka. Still others are out hawking their wares at flea markets. They steal a little, sell a little, deal a little—in short, they find a way to live by puttering about.

Moscow is literally swarming with such self-styled vendors. The same is true of other cities in Russia. But each time I peer into the faces of these vendors, I ask myself this question: Each of these people, standing with their humble wares set out on newspapers and crates, didn't they used to be somebody else? They were once workers, engineers, teachers, collective farmers, scientists in research institutes. . . . Nevertheless they left their professions, their well-worn niches—and for what? So this is where those superintellectual characters and readers of Ludmilla Petrushevskaya, the popular Russian novelist, have gone. Here they are in the same rows as the plump middle-aged ladies from Ukraine selling pork fat and blood sausage, next to skilled workers from factories stalled by conversion, alongside destitute old ladies from the bankrupt ghost towns outside of Moscow, with the unfortunate Muscovite pensioners, for whom each day endured is like the battle of Stalingrad.

Although these people have chopped off their old roots, they have not grown new ones. They cannot become real merchants because they don't have their own stores, vending places, or wholesale outlets. They have no regular customers nor their own business. All of this "retail" is haphazard—someone buys something a little cheaper, sells it for a little more, and either spends the difference or puts it back into circulation. They do not pay taxes and no one registers them—except perhaps the mafia, which has long arms and a big appetite. They have no legal status or defense. Such commerce cannot guarantee reliable and safe earnings. And if you take into account the bribes (and the beatings) from the police and the racketeers, at times they are worse off than when they started. Nevertheless, half of Russia is selling. And half of Russia is buying. Nobody is producing. In 1993, 42 percent of the retail trade went through "shuttlers" who travel abroad to buy goods to resell, through private persons, or through unregistered companies.

All of this comprises the so-called "gray" economy. It is gray because essentially all the products sold are contraband. Forty-two percent of retail a year—that's an enormous figure! Let us imagine how these figures could coincide with the percentages of Russians who are "below the poverty line." Perhaps this is the reason that no one is fainting and falling down from hunger even though they do not receive their wages for months, or receive far less than the minimum living standard? People have found a second niche for themselves: extra earnings in the shadow economy.

The most amazing thing is that this is not merely a means of survival, a way of preventing death by starvation, a temporary phenomenon. No one even dreams of returning to their old lives when things settle down. These people find their new mode of existence quite to their taste because they don't have to put any labor into such vending. They do not have to do anything or produce anything. They do not have to work with their hands or their head. All that is required is to stand next to their wares and name a price. Zero effort. You buy, you sell, you get money. It used to be illegal, now it's allowed. It is a mixture of hackwork and freeloading sanctioned by the government. And if you don't feel like standing out in the freezing cold, there is something even simpler: invest money in stocks and securities. True, for the sake of collecting your dividends, you have to get yourself crushed in lines, but that's almost a form of entertainment.

Of course, not all of these people turned to vending because of the traditional Russian idleness—many of them were driven to it from desperation. After all, when you're paid pennies or nothing at all and you have hungry children at home, most likely you are willing to do almost anything. Most likely.

The reform began more than four years ago. Perestroika, which actually started everything, also took about three years. All together it has been about seven years. How could Russian society reach such a state in such a short time? How could our social ties break so easily, and the moral foundations crumble? The answer is clear: The ties were unstable to begin with and the foundations were extremely shaky. Today's lumpens did not arise out of a vacuum—they were bred from yesterday's marginals.

It is enough to recall what happened to Russia at the turn of the century to understand that truly ideal conditions were created here for the emergence of enormous masses of marginals, these "interim people," and their ensuing lumpenization. First came World War I, then the October Revolution of 1917, then the Civil War and emigration. Next came War Communism, collectivization, and industrialization. This enormous country occupying one-sixth of the earth's land surface bubbled like an enormous pot, mixing millions and millions of people in frenzied vortexes, disrupting customary ties, sweeping masses of people like grains of sand in the sea from one place to another. Stalin's purges, the forced resettlement of peoples, and World War II only finished off the dissolution of social ties. Through all this, the best of the best perished, the very ones who had stood out from the gray masses.

Already by the time of the Khrushchev-Brezhnev era there existed in the USSR a special "ghetto" subculture, as scholars called it, with a new type of déclassé loafer who remained within the framework of his social group. In the perestroika and reform eras the formation of this sociopsychological type was completed. Now a new pyramid of power has been created, and those who have come up from the bottom, yesterday's bums and loafers, have carried the psychology of the freeloader to the top—and to all segments of the new society.

Freeloaders are ruled by the psychology of the mob. The Russian mob, ordinarily an extremely passive swamp, has an inert but terrible strength and needs a leader. If the mob is swayed or stirred, if the dangerous wave is skillfully raised, it is capable of washing over, drowning, and sweeping away everything in its path. Just as happened in 1917. Just as happened in the December 1993 elections when Russia unexpectedly elected Zhirinovsky.

In the first year of the Great Reform, Moscow swarmed with empty-pot marches and hungry-line processions.* Now the sign of the times is different: crowds of duped people swell the central streets of cities, indignantly demanding their money back. These are the crowds of the failed post-Soviet investors, players, or partners—call them what you will. As a rule they do not get their money back, the con men having safely disappeared over the horizon with other people's billions and trillions in their pockets. The scandal in the newspaper gradually dies down without having had any visible effect; as soon as the passions quiet down millions of Russian dreamers once again start wondering where they should put their savings. They want to be rich, and why not? The television commercial promises it, and we believe it.

Of course not all of the investors are simply loafers and parasites. You cannot discount the really needy, for example the single old ladies who have scraped together a hundred dollars for their own funerals and have decided to invest them somewhere so as to somehow make it to their deaths. There are quite a few of these elderly women, all of whom, incidentally, are noted for a high degree of voting activity—a deeply rooted habit from the Soviet era when voting was mandatory. Populist leaders take this fact into account.

---

* Demonstrations allegedly populated by hungry people who had been waiting in lines outside stores, or who were carrying empty pots and pans. Some suspected that these demonstrators were paid or bused to rallies by the opposition.—TRANS.

Meanwhile Alisa the Fox and Bazilio the Cat in all their incarnations cajole and lure and coax from television screens, newspaper ads, and the street, urging the foolish Pinnochios to bury their money in the Russian field of miracles so that an enormous tree bearing shiny new gold pieces—or even better, "little green ones" (as American dollars are lovingly nicknamed)—will grow overnight. Those longing for money who can't wait and "want it right now," gamble in all sorts of games and lotteries—a type of casino for the poor. Theoretically the chances are great and the risk to your pocket is insignificant.

One especially popular weekly game show on television is even called *Field of Miracles*. The object is to guess a word, sometimes a ridiculously easy one, after getting clues. For example, "a carnivorous mammal" might be the clue for *hyena*. The players and the audience are not known for their brilliance, to put it bluntly. (In order to get on the show you supposedly have to submit your own crossword puzzle as part of a contest but I suspect that like everywhere else in Russia some fixing and connections are required.) Wrinkling their brows, torturously rolling their eyes, and breaking out in a sweat, five players try to guess the letters in the word. My daughter, sitting in front of the television at home, gets the word right off the bat.

While the game show contestants are thinking up a storm, the arrow on a roulette wheel stops on the sector marked *Prize*.

"Will you keep playing or go for the prize?" asks the host.

"I'll take the prize," the contestant says greedily.

"Bring the prize into the studio!" cries the host dramatically. His name is Yakubovich and he is a brilliant actor of God-given talent. His wise, all-seeing, all-understanding eyes are those of an old rabbi, full of hidden sorrow. There is no contempt, but only pity for these unfortunate people and for himself, obliged to work at such a silly job. But the situation dictates it, and he urges enthusiastically, "Applause, audience!"

People begin clapping wildly in anticipation of their favorite spectacle: a prize brought into the studio in a black box. No one knows what's inside since the box itself is not very large and contains only the name of the prize on a piece of paper. Now the circus act begins, performed by Yakubovich with true virtuosity. He starts to bargain as if at the marketplace in Odessa. "So what do you pick, the prize or the money?" he asks provocatively, like the serpent tempter.

"The prize," the contestant says, holding his ground.

"And what if I were to offer you half a million rubles ($250)! Would you take it?" Yakubovich persists. An expression of suffering appears on the contestant's face. After all, he doesn't know what's written on the paper in the damned box—"Panasonic television" or "head of cabbage."

"How about one and a half million rubles? Two million! Don't be sorry, now," Yakubovich teases. And the game player breaks down.

"The money!" he decides greedily.

Two bags are brought into the studio. One contains two million rubles (a very large sum for our times—almost $1000, when the average monthly wage is $110). The other holds donuts. Outwardly the packages are completely indistinguishable. If you make a mistake, you'll wind up with— as we say in Russia—a donut hole. Actually nobody goes home empty-handed. The show has rich sponsors interested in advertising their products, so the losers will still leave with at least some kind of souvenir, either a tape player, a set of compact discs, perfume, or another such trinket.

Throughout the show the Super Prize—the unattainable dream of every Russian, a new foreign car—revolves on a slowly turning dais, as in a fairy-tale crystal palace, sending the audience into trembles of delight at its gleaming, varnished panels and chrome details. Each time the host looks over at *it*, each time he makes mention of *it*, the audience gasps. But the Super Prize can only be won in the Super Game, in which one contestant faces the tricky, mysterious final word all alone. (It does actually happen: I once saw a winner get into his brand-new Peugeot and wheel home right out of the studio. The only thing I don't know is whether it was all won fair and square, but that didn't seem to bother the audience.)

Finally all the hyenas and dogs and cats have been guessed, the winner has been determined, and it's time for the Super Game. And the Super Prize. THE CAR. The audience is absolutely silent. All that can be heard is the sound of their hearts thumping. At home there's the same deafening pounding. Half of Russia is avidly glued to their television screens, waiting.

A skinny old fellow from somewhere in Ukraine who has beat the other contestants in guessing *hyena* gives the impression that he is not only a mental lightweight but completely illiterate. It's not clear how he ever managed to make up the crossword puzzle required for the contest. He is happy and proud, simply bursting with his good fortune. Wiping away his sweat and tears with a handkerchief, he reads out some verses of his own composition devoted to the *Field of Miracles* game and to the host Yakubovich personally. Yakubovich sweeps away a phony tear. But now comes the sacred moment of truth. The word must be guessed on the first try, after being given only one letter. The first letter is "H." The clue is "a character in ancient Greek mythology."

"I'll give you a hint," says the host sympathetically, looking at the purple face of the old man, who looks as if he's about to have a stroke from the tension and the worry. Clearly this word is over his head. "This person in Greek mythology is the daughter of one of the sea gods."

The face of the old contestant grows even more gloomy, then suddenly lights up. "Hamlet!" he cries joyfully.

In the studio nobody laughs. Nobody has understood the idiocy of his answer. Everyone tensely awaits Yakubovich's reaction. Go figure, maybe it really is Hamlet? Those at home who are a little better educated are no doubt falling off their chairs with laughter.

Yakubovich, of course, knows better, but he's not chuckling. He is the picture of sorrow. He knows everything—both the right answers and the dense illiteracy of the contestants—but he remains tactfully silent. Perhaps he really does pity the old man.

"No," Yakubovich intones mournfully. "Unfortunately, you guessed wrong. The answer is Harpy, who in Greek mythology was the daughter of the sea deity Taumant and the ocean goddess Elektra. So the main prize remains in the studio! Let's give him a hand!"

The crowd cautiously applauds because they know that this is still not the end.

"But for your courage in playing, *Field of Miracles* is giving you a consolation prize, a Sony video tape player!"

Upon hearing this the studio breaks out in shouts and roars. People jump up from their seats yelling and screaming. Now it was all according to the rules. Here it was, the longed-for moment! The taste of victory! Long live *Field of Miracles*! What a great thing it was, the freebie!

Thus before the eyes of the whole country the myth that anyone can get rich, at least a little bit rich, without working comes convincingly to life. That night feverish television viewers dream of crystal palaces on the shores of the ocean, filled with free Sony televisions, Peugeots, and Polaroid cameras. Then when they get up in the morning and look with loathing at the walls of their run-down little apartments, they come out on the street with the determined desire to catch—right away, today, without putting it off until later—that temptingly close, but for some reason always elusive Firebird of Fortune. Meanwhile everything already lies in wait for the Firebird hunters. The snares have been set and the bird itself has been tied up nearby as a decoy.

At literally every entrance to the metro and in every underground passageway there are people sitting with megaphones, calling loudly to pedestrians, like sweet-voiced sirens, not to pass by their happiness. Those who have already been burned once hurry on; the unenlightened slow their pace. "Buy just one Supersprint lottery ticket," sing the sirens, "and in one minute you will be the happy possessor of one million American dollars! Wins up to $100 are paid on the spot. If you buy ten tickets at once and don't win on a single one, you get your money back! Just scratch off the ticket, and you're a millionaire!"

The pedestrians' eyes burn brightly and their hands crawl automatically toward their wallets. The thrill of gambling! However the sirens don't tell you that they are violating regulations when they sell Supersprint tickets, or Chernobyl Children raffles (a charity), or Super-Nevada chances. First, the price in rubles is three times what it is supposed to be. Second, the buyer who falls for the vendors' transparent marketing gimmick and immediately buys up ten tickets is in for a very unpleasant surprise—it is virtually certain that one of the tickets will be a small winner of a dollar so that he won't get any money back.

At least these tickets are something you can feel, smell, and bite with your teeth. If after you've scratched off the ticket, you find the Firebird has once again flown past you, well, at least it's *your* bad luck and *your* loss. It's painful, yet fair. But there are cases when not only the Firebird but the tickets themselves are as vaporous as a mirage, and weary ticket buyers will never see the lottery drawings because they never take place. The scam artists have long since disappeared with their loot.

If they wish, thrillseekers have an opportunity to stimulate their nerves with more than sponsored gambling. I can recommend a few more original ways. For example, one can risk buying a car or apartment on credit.

A recent and very typical example was the Vlastilina scandal in a Moscow suburb. Vlastilina sold cars on time at low prices. Tens of thousands of buyers (including highly paid officials) who collectively put down many millions of dollars, were left holding the bag when the company folded. They went looking for the director with dogs, but couldn't find her. With that kind of money scammers in any country would be hard to find. The funniest thing was that almost the entire local police department had plunked down their savings with this company!

The celebrated characters of MMM's commercial spots, Lyonya Golubkov and the single woman Marina Sergeyevna (by the way, thanks to her MMM shares, she found a suitor) just couldn't be beat. The "smart" father and son advertising the Telemarket shares went on fishing and punching their calculators. ("We're sitting here, and the money's working for us.") The irritating, obnoxious characters from the Hoper-Invest company kept announcing that "Everybody loves Hoper!" The Selenga Trading House went on expressing its concern about Russia's riches, and the Chara commercial bank and the Tibet Concern, where until recently all of Moscow's art and performance world was "grazing," continued to swear to their honesty on television. It would take forever to count all these outfits.

All of them have shamelessly lied, lured, and enticed, and the suckers were simply waiting to be hooked. They were so desperate for easy money! And really, if a company doesn't disappear overnight along with its chairman, the first investors do still manage to get some sort of return, which whips up the agitation of the masses. But as the cash collected grows, the inevitable unhappy ending approaches: either bankruptcy is declared, the director flees the country with other people's money, or the accounts are frozen for the unforeseeable future. The investment funds and joint-stock companies then play the ubiquitous game of lowering their quotations. All of this generally corresponds to the popular Russian proverb: The horse radish is no sweeter than the radish; that is, it's six of one and half a dozen of the other.

A month, even a week doesn't go by in Moscow without a furor breaking out over a scam or a bankruptcy in credit and finance operations. The first to go bust are those firms that attracted the savings of people with modest means—the state employees, the retirees, and the war veterans—in exchange for promises of fixed dividends, superhigh interest rates, premium payments, and all sorts of bonuses. By the most cautious calculations, from January 1993 through May 1994 con men were able to swindle no fewer than a million Muscovites. Among the victims are people who have been burned three or four times before but keep trying to catch that elusive Firebird. I have an acquaintance who has already contrived to close down three such companies. Either she has bad karma or just a bad eye, but the fact of the matter is that no sooner does she invest her last savings somewhere than the firm is "told it doesn't have long to live." There is another Russian saying: Whoever doesn't take a risk, doesn't drink champagne. But nowadays the opposite is true in Russia. Some take the risk, but others drink the champagne.

The winter of 1993 began with the Tekhnoprogress scandal, and it went on from there, never stopping. Pyramid schemers in Russia are free to do as they please because the system for licensing such firms has always been tenuous. Only about a dozen such enterprises are licensed by the Central Bank. The others don't have licenses and don't intend to obtain them, registering sometimes with false ID, and sometimes using other people's documents—even without the knowledge of the real holder of the ID. In March and April 1994 alone, no less than six firms folded, along with their investors' nest eggs. Next came even more outrageous stories about the certificate investment fund called Neft-

Almaz-Invest (*neft* is the word for oil in Russia, and *almaz* means diamond), the Tibet Concern, the Selenga Trading House, and others. But MMM has outdone them all.

All of this took place in the summer of 1994 at the height of the vacation season. The president of MMM, Sergei Mavrodi, claims that MMM has forty-five to fifty million investors. This is virtually impossible to verify since the accounts are not named, but experts in the field and the media cite another, far more modest figure—about a million shareholders. Even a million true believers fired up with the crazy idea of getting rich through MMM—that's an awful lot! It's almost a political party—the Freeloader Party, as journalists have sarcastically dubbed it.

If you take the members of this "party" to the barricades, or merely to the ballot boxes (and for the sake of their freebie money they'll come running—you don't even have to promise them free vodka), what will you get? There isn't a single Russian party today that could dream of that kind of success.

The MMM scandal blew up suddenly; no one was expecting this turn of affairs. The commercial recounting the dizzying rise and prosperity of the company of the Golubkovs kept assaulting our eyes and ears, flashing on the television screen a dozen times an evening. Every day hundreds of new converts would take their last gold pieces to the MMM share offices.

I missed the very beginning of the story. My daughter and I were in Sochi and only learned from the newspapers that the government had "swooped down"—that's the fashionable phrase for it now—on MMM. I did manage to see the scene of the arrest of MMM's president, Mavrodi, on television in Moscow. It all looked fairly strange, if not comical. When they came to handcuff him, the chairman of the "people's joint-stock company" was sitting quietly at home, although he didn't open the door. The riot police were already standing outside, and Mavrodi was demonstratively destroying documents. In his office were one and a half million dollars in unaccounted-for cash. Could he really have failed to spirit away the money earlier? Certainly the scandal had been brewing for a week by that time. The impression was that Mavrodi simply *wanted* to be arrested.

As a result the riot police, wearing black masks just like in the gangster movies, crawled into his apartment from the balcony and grabbed him as he sat quietly waiting for them. Now wearing a martyr's crown of thorns, he walked out of the house, resigning himself to the "government's abuse" and got into the police car, regally waving to the crowd of "partners." He was utterly unperturbed and knew exactly what he was doing. He wanted to show the whole world that it was the *government* that was getting its paws on people's hard-earned money. He remained silent about the fact that MMM's stock quotations had plummeted to almost zero. It was *them*, the government bureaucrats, who were to blame, and not MMM, and certainly not Mavrodi himself—a kind capitalist with a human face.

Ultimately Mavrodi was charged with tax evasion. In fact it wasn't MMM itself that had failed to pay its taxes, but a spin-off firm, Invest-Consulting. Thus the government had no reason to close down MMM and stop payments to the public; the government would not commit such a stupid act. It was Mavrodi himself who ordered the doors shut, which whipped up the angry crowds—but with the result that Mavrodi became a popular avenger and martyr, and the government officials looked like tyrants and villains. Mr. Zhirinovsky himself, chairman of the Liberal Democratic Party, came out in support of Mavrodi, and some hot-heads in the State Duma even called for appointing this financial wiz the minister of finance.

All of this gave the impression of a carefully planned and quite clever game. Sergei Mavrodi is indeed an unusual individual. He really did have a marvelous knack for counting—especially cards and money. He learned it when he was still a young man studying at the Moscow Institute of Electronic Machine-Building (now the Moscow State Institute of Electronics and Mathematics) in the department of applied mathematics. Even then he was fascinated with games of chance—solitaire and business, which is a game, too, is it not? (Only at the time, it was simply called *fartsovka*, that is, dealing on the black market. According to the media he sold jeans, records, and cassettes.)

This unusual individual brilliantly figured out Russian psychology, putting his finger on what would bring a crowd of people to him: the age-old dream of something for nothing. Each MMM commercial is, like Pushkin's "Little Tragedies," a psychological masterpiece. Mavrodi did not show the public rich and well-fed people, thereby angering them with the contrast to their own lives. He showed the public itself, as in a mirror—half bum, half lumpen; impoverished and wretched; someone to whom he, the benefactor, gave a chance to become a person. A person he did not disdain (the government and the major banks did)—but had paid the honor of taking in as a *partner*! The intelligentsia could wail and gnash its teeth as much as it wanted along with all its mass media. The *people* liked it. And the people brought their money. And the people trusted Mavrodi like their own father and believed that being a "partner" of

MMM was the only way of surviving in a state where you had been deceived. All the more because the president of MMM was not shy with his promises and offered rapid, universal prosperity. Once again, however, the good life didn't materialize. Once again the rainbow-colored soap bubble, blown up to incredible proportions, burst.

What in fact did happen? There were quite a few versions of the story of who profited from MMM's collapse. The newspapers claimed that MMM had been "set up" by its competitors because Mavrodi was a lone wolf who didn't want to share with anyone. It was said that the authorities had gotten revenge because he had siphoned the public's funds away from the Central Bank (which is absolute nonsense, since the Central Bank never accepted private deposits in the first place and the siphoning off of funds would have even helped the government from the perspective of slowing the pace of inflation). It was said that other rival organizations were concerned about MMM's expansionist policy, although it had begun on a peripheral financial market. Or that the government deliberately provoked the inevitable collapse of MMM to let off steam in the summer while everyone was on vacation.

Whatever the case, the turn of events was very much to the advantage of Mavrodi himself. By jacking up the artificial quotations to 13,000 rubles (almost $4.50) per share, MMM had reached the point where the ordinary "partner" could no longer afford the shares. Moreover, MMM didn't have the funds to pay out on them; after all from the very beginning MMM had been built on a pyramid scheme, paying old investors only at the expense of new "partners."

While MMM's president, beloved by the people,

cooled his heels in jail without experiencing any particular deprivations, his "partners," consumed with grief, wrote letters to the newspapers (some claim that these publications were paid for rather handsomely). I will cite a few of these masterpieces of the epistolic genre published in the August issues of *Izvestia*. Even though they were fabricated from beginning to end by Mavrodi's own skillful team of psychologists and paid for out of MMM's coffers, they reflect what the thousands of duped Golubkovs were thinking and saying. In other words, if these letters had not been invented, they would have had to have existed.

> Dear Respected Founder of MMM,
>
> I am very grateful that at least you are concerned about the welfare of simple people. Our stupid government and our "respected" president are only concerned about how to turn the screws tighter and stop up the loopholes so that an ordinary person can't manage to get even some kind of income. They just need to stuff their own wallets even fuller. I couldn't understand why they didn't like the commercial that showed that a simple working person could live alongside their families, their children, and themselves. We are supposed to work in their homes like servants, but we aren't supposed to have anything of our own. They write that MMM is speculation and fraud. But why don't they say that they themselves are defrauding people, and badly? They are lowering inflation by not paying wages. They are building palaces on the money of ordinary people and their families are living abroad.
>
> By organizing the persecution of MMM, they want a social explosion. Thankfully there are still hon-

est, pure, and just people in our country—like the foun-
der of MMM.

Respectfully yours,

Vasilchenko
(Novosibirsk)

Dear MMM,

I have been a shareholder of yours for several
months. I bought my first shares after getting my sever-
ance pay when I was laid off from work. Only your
shares have enabled me and my children not to die of
starvation—we have no other income. Everything that
was left after the death of my parents, all of their
savings—everything!—was devalued by the government. . . .

I completely believe in the honesty of MMM
and its president, Sergei Mavrodi, but I heartily doubt
the decency of all of our "kings for a day" who are at
the helm of power in Russia.

Therefore if you need my help with anything—
writing letters somewhere, demonstrating in defense of
MMM against provocations by the government—in any
event you can call on me.

Galina Ter-Mikaelyan
(Podolsk)

One of the journalists ascerbically remarked, "If, day
after day, as in a mirror, they show the people to be an idiot
and smile while doing it, then this people is simply doomed
to elect Zhirinovsky."[10] But the people, our Great and Mighty
People, have gone even further. Once again they have proved
that no political scientist or commentator is capable of pen-

etrating their mysterious depths. This time it was not Zhirinovsky they elected, but Mavrodi with his crown of thorns
—a man under investigation put right into the parliament!

Mavrodi was released by authorities in a panic immediately after the collapse of the ruble on Black Tuesday,
October 11, 1994. They were afraid of a social explosion, but
why jail him and then let him out right on the eve of the
elections in Mytishchinsky District where Mavrodi had run
for deputy to the State Duma? Perhaps there were some
invisible strings behind all this. Whatever the case, they got
themselves a little present—a new member of the parliament
who also happened to be a tax dodger to the tune of 49.9
billion rubles. I ask you, where, in what other country of the
world, would such a thing be possible?!

On the eve of the elections Mavrodi himself, without
batting an eyelash, announced, "If you do not elect me,
they'll put me in jail again. Then I cannot fulfill my promises
to the investors."

At the very end of October, then, elections took place
in Mytishchinsky District where the parliamentary seat trag-
ically had been left vacant by the murder of Deputy Aid-
zerzis. Sergei Mavrodi, the MMM president in disgrace, won
the day, beating out Konstantin Borovoy, a wealthy commodities trader and chairman of the Party of Economic
Freedom, and additional opponents—a supporter of fascist
leaders, a person close to the murdered "godfather" Kvan-
trishvili, and others. Never mind that Mavrodi garnered just
shy of 29 percent of those who bothered to turn out for the
elections (mainly retirees and the poor). Never mind that, as
some malicious gossips claimed, outrageous abuses were tol-
erated in conducting the election campaign itself, and that
Mavrodi's supporters supposedly paid up to 40,000 rubles to

those who voted for him. What was important was that Mavrodi won, and that the Freeloader Party that did not yet exist *de jure*, but *de facto*, had been chosen.

Mavrodi's party, as has become only too clear recently, not only wields powerful lobbying leverage in parliament, it possesses a far weightier influence on the course of political events in the country than, for example, the major banks. The figures cited in the August 1994 issues of *Izvestia* are staggering: about half of surveyed Muscovites (46 percent) are owners of shares in various stock companies and funds. The number of MMM shareholders, as the calculations showed, reached 7 percent of the population of Moscow. Seven percent is quite a number (although shares of the Hermes Group are owned by 14 percent of the population). It is at least half a million voters. Taking into account the shareholders from Russia's other regions, it is quite likely that MMM could gather the million signatures needed to conduct a referendum. If we include Zhirinovsky's electorate, who spoke out fervently on Mavrodi's behalf and who actively monitored the elections in Mytishchinsky District, then what kind of numbers are we talking about? And what is behind it?

Why did the voters choose Mavrodi? Because he paid up to 40,000 rubles per vote? That has yet to be proven. Because he promised to pay MMM's debts to investors? Because he pledged to give $100 million to Mytishchinsky District? That's all true—but only a part of the reason. The main stimulus was the idea of getting something for nothing. Strange, but an idea nonetheless—the new pragmatism of the Russian man in the street. Sergei Buntman, a commentator for the Moscow radio station Echo Moscow, formulated this idea quite astutely:

They fought for a new, pragmatic idealism, for a thread, a piece of paper, a symbol, a game. The government doesn't provide anything and doesn't create jobs. Life forces them to do everything themselves. Then along comes a great, wonderful, million-billion dollar illusion and occupation, and profit from one's own bother and one's own efforts. A voucher—what's that? You invested, tried to get something back, got burned, and forgot about it. But now there's MMM who, like the Wizard of Oz, gives you green spectacles, and all the pieces of glass turn into emeralds. What do you care that it's an illusion! Are there emeralds? There are. Are they valued? They are. Who cares that it's only in one city. Do they exchange them for money? They do. And if you take off the glasses, it's not the Wizard's fault. It's the fault of the Wicked Witch of the East and her soldiers.[11]

The Freeloaders Party isn't so mythological after all. Literally within a few days after his election to the State Duma, Sergei Mavrodi founded a parliamentary group with sixteen members. It is called the Party of People's Capital, and its chairman—a capitalist with a human face—has expressed a wish to work in the parliament's security council. An interesting combination—Mavrodi's money plus Zhirinovsky's votes. Before you know it there'll be early elections for the president of Russia.

Chapter 8

The Russian Woman

The cover of a recent Western book about Russia features a picture of the Old Arbat, one of the liveliest streets in central Moscow. Looming large in the foreground is a young but terribly overweight Russian woman in a hideous flowered dress, carrying the traditional "just-in-case" net bag from which protrudes a stick of sausage. Two things surprised me about this photograph: the tenacity of the Western stereotype of the Soviet (and now simply Russian) woman and the photographer's good luck in managing to find a live example of this stereotype.

I say "good luck" because there really aren't such ugly, unkempt "rural" women in Moscow these days, nor out in the sticks, nor in the large provincial cities. Russian women have always been famous for their beauty and now that they have finally obtained good makeup and pretty, stylish clothing, you wouldn't recognize them. But the changes that brought perestroika and reform have not only affected the face and figure of the Russian woman; more importantly, they have touched her heart and soul.

ᴄᴏ

In the old USSR, popular songs were devoted to collective farm women, weavers, and tractor drivers—the ideal Soviet women. Times have changed dramatically, along with the songs and of course the women of Russia themselves. They have not gone back to the image of Turgenev's elegant lady, romantic and otherwordly, but neither are they reminiscent of the statue of the collective farm woman soaring above the National Economic Achievements Exhibit in Moscow—a mighty bronze dame with sturdy calves and firm buttocks. Nor are they like the Komsomol girls of the 1920s, or the Party activists in the mannish jackets of the Brezhnev era. No, they are remarkably diverse, these new women, although they all live in the same country. Their differences depend largely on their degree of wealth and consequently their lifestyle.

There are four types of working women in Russia today. The first type, the standard, is the "workhorse," who is not necessarily a blue-collar worker, but perhaps someone with a higher degree. With equal zeal she carries two burdens—work and family—wearing herself out to earn a piece of bread and create some elementary comfort in the home, something achieved only through superhuman efforts because of the constant shortage of cash. Unfortunately these women make up the majority. You can always immediately pick a "workhorse" out of the crowd. She stands out among her carefree, happy, and relaxed girlfriends because of the worried, almost hunted expression in her eyes—even if they are heavily made up—the stress lines on her still-youthful brow, and her frenetic pace. She is always hurrying somewhere, and is always late, torn among a thousand duties. Her stylish purse inevitably contains a carefully folded plastic bag for the groceries she will buy somewhere on the fly—the modern successor of the "just-in-case" net bag.

The second type of woman is exotic—the creative type. Often she has no family, or if she does, it is a truncated version of one (she's a single mother) or is modified (she, her child, and an excuse of a lover who fills in for a husband). Despite the burdens of life, she is true to her ideals and continues to create, even on her ridiculously low salary. Those who are particularly beautiful or fortunate sometimes grasp a straw in the person of a rich patron—like the pre-revolutionary ladies, the "camellias."

The third type is pragmatic. These are the professional "easy women," or girls without any hangups. Their life now is a constant winning lottery and the envy of the younger generation. But not everyone has the necessary attributes for this category, and not all beauties are prepared to take this road.

That leaves the fourth type, the so-called new career woman. These include a diverse range of black-marketeers, workers in the newly privatized sector of trade and services, entrepreneurs, and political and public figures.

Since the majority of Russian women are in the first category, I'll start with them.

∾

I have an acquaintance named Masha, a typical "workhorse." She is thirty-six years old, very nice and even pretty, but often unhappy. I often visit her and have the opportunity to observe her everyday life practically from the inside. I have come to the conclusion that if one were to write a novel on the hero of *our* time,* Masha would be an ideal prototype. The scenario might go like this:

Masha's day began with the obnoxious buzz of the alarm clock. Seven o'clock, time to get up. That buzz always ruined Masha's mood. By nature a night owl, she could not get to sleep early, no matter how she tried—she got caught up in housework, sat up in front of the television, and before she knew it, the night had flown by.

Through an effort of will, overcoming the temptation to stuff the alarm clock under a pillow, Masha, sullen and irritated, threw a housecoat over her nightgown and shuffled to the kitchen to make breakfast. Her husband continued to sleep soundly—obviously, making breakfast, washing dishes, doing the laundry, buying groceries, packing the children off to school or day care, and other such nonsense wasn't a man's job. Just what *was* a man's job exactly, except in bed (which, because of exhaustion, happened less and less often), Masha had already ceased to understand, because her husband earned hardly any more than she did—if not less. She had already stopped reproaching him for his lack of help around the house; she had tried, but each time it would end in an ugly quarrel so now she didn't bother and conserved her nerves. Meanwhile her husband continued to demand his male privileges, behaving like an Asian shah in his harem.

Now that he had finally risen from bed, it never occurred to him to make it. He got dressed and turned on the

---

* The famous novella of the nineteenth-century writer Mikhail Lermontov was entitled *Hero of Our Time.*—Trans.

television news while reading the paper, waiting for his breakfast to be served. He read in silence, not getting into any conversation with his wife, who banged pots and pans around in annoyance.

At one time Masha had loved her husband very much. He was handsome, good-natured, and witty, and a promising graduate student in chemistry. But as the years went by, her hopes were not justified, and her husband had somehow faded and grown dim and flabby at forty years. He was always grumbling, which irritated Masha to no end, straining as she did under the weight of her numerous responsibilities. Her girlfriends all envied her; her husband seemed like a real treasure. He didn't drink, didn't smoke, didn't philander, and was at home every night by eight o'clock. Masha didn't share their enthusiasm because she knew that her husband was an absolutely unnecessary and useless object in the background, like a detail in the wallpaper.

Sometimes she thought it would have been better not to have married at all, but what could she do now? Two children—a boy, five, and a girl already in school—who needed a father, at least some kind of father. Masha herself had been raised without a father and remembered all too well the horrible despair when people asked her about her daddy. She was already staring forty in the face and finding that life wasn't all it was cracked up to be. Having borne two children and having stayed home until they started school or day care (she didn't have parents to help with the kids, as did some fortunate women), Masha had missed her chance. With her degree in philology and knowledge of two languages (already forgotten with the passing of the years), she was of no use to anyone.

Thus Masha was forced to work as a proofreader at a publishing house that had fallen on hard times. The job wasn't working-class, but not considered part of the world of the creative intelligentsia, either—or even a white-collar job as such—she wasn't sure what to call it. It was dull, monotonous work, but had to be endured, because at least they paid regularly, every month. Her husband worked in an engineering office where he headed some ridiculous and useless laboratory where no one had been paid for six months. It was a state-subsidized bureau that had previously been part of the military-industrial complex. God knew what they did in that laboratory now; ever since conversion, research had almost ground to a halt. Her husband preferred to keep his own council, but from a few off-hand remarks Masha had long ago figured out that no work was going on there. Mostly the employees sat around drinking tea, playing chess, gossiping, smoking themselves blue in the face, discussing political news, and intriguing against one another.

Masha had hinted to her husband repeatedly that it would be a good idea to do something useful—the children were growing up, after all, and needed clothing and books, and what with groceries getting more expensive every day, there was barely enough cash. But each time she broached the subject, her husband, puffing himself up arrogantly like a peacock, announced that he considered it shameful to sell things on the market. On the whole he didn't have a head for business—he'd never studied it. That was certainly true, Masha was forced to concede. We were all taught something else, but somehow you had to make a living!

Just look at her girlfriend Lusya's husband who had started trading in raw materials and had opened up a little company—so that in a few months they had bought a Japanese television, an Italian washing machine, and now were saving to buy some imported furniture. Only a year ago there hadn't been enough to buy food. Lusya was no longer working, just going around to cosmetic salons and beauty parlors pampering her ethereal beauty. Obviously her husband was in cahoots with the mafia—some suspicious types were constantly hanging around their apartment; they had installed a steel door and a locked safe in their home along with a vicious watchdog, and his partner was nearly blown up in his car recently. So this new success was an entirely dubious form of good fortune.

Hastily cutting up some bread, cheese, and boiled sausage (they always used to eat smoked sausage for breakfast, but now the prices were too painful), Masha brewed some tea and watched the water bubble in the pot to boil some eggs. Actually there was no need for her to stand at the stove guarding the boiling water—it was just a kind of ruse, an opportunity to get at least a minute alone to herself and put her thoughts and feelings together. Reality was right nearby, after all: her eternally disgruntled husband, irritatingly rustling his newspaper pages, her ugly apartment; her noisy children who were constantly demanding things— money, presents, or sweets—and not gladdening her with any achievements or model behavior. All that was understandable—the children were just being children—but when a forty-year-old man began throwing a tantrum like a child, Masha had a fervent desire to bang something heavy over her husband's head.

Absently gazing at the bubbling water rising from the pot, Masha abstractedly and even without any particular sorrow reflected on her girlfriends' lives in her mind.

There was Nina, a girl she used to go to school with,

who wasn't doing too badly. She had given up teaching at the university, for which she was being paid pennies, and had found a job as a secretary in a foreign company. Her lover got her in since he was a manager, and now Nina was getting $500 a month—a very comfortable salary. She had enough for everything—herself, her child, and even her husband who, like Masha's husband, was a confirmed idler. Her husband knew about her lover, but chose to look the other way; the wife was bringing money home, and that was a good thing. Recently the couple had gone to Majorca on vacation—naturally on her dime.

Another girlfriend, Nadya, did not work, but lived off her interest (her husband was given a disability pension after an operation). Nadya invested $3,000 in various banks and financial companies—money she had earned at the expense of her health (she suffered from asthma and, since she worked as a monumental artist and had to use varnishes and paints, had nearly headed off to the next world.) She spent whole weeks running from one line to the next to pick up her dividends. The other day one of the banks where she had invested $1,500 in hard currency froze its accounts, so she was mourning the loss of her cash.

And what about that other girlfriend, Mila? Her husband was pretty rich, one of the "new Russians"—but as experience has shown, rich husbands do not make faithful husbands: as soon as they start earning some easy money, it's drinking, carousing, and women. Masha had already seen enough examples of this, and perhaps for that reason wasn't pushing her own husband too hard into such underground work. The rich husband almost never gave his wife much money, never took her out with him, and had fixed himself up with a bevy of young lovers. Even so Mila put up with it all. What other choice did she have? Of course she could get a divorce, but what would she do by herself—alone with a child, without education or a profession?

Yes, it was always something. The rich had one set of problems; the poor another (Masha placed herself in the middle somewhere). Take her neighbor downstairs. She worked at one factory, and her husband worked at another. A day didn't go by without a drunken spree in their house. Whenever her husband got drunk he'd start punching out anybody who got in his way. If a stool came to hand, he'd hit someone with it, or if it was an iron, he'd fling it at someone. How many times the police had come to their door! Not surprisingly, with a home life like that, the daughter became a prostitute—she'd run away to anywhere, do anything, just so she didn't have to look at all that and depend on her family financially.

Obviously there's a plethora of such Russian women these days. They are eternally unhappy, whether poor or rich, smart or stupid, dogs or lookers. It's the rare woman in Russia these days who has a happy family life.

Of course you can use men, as does Sonya, a striking blonde who drives them simply mad. She just extracts money from them. Once Masha saw Sonya's latest sugar daddy, a fat toad—she couldn't understand how Sonya could get into bed with him. No, selling herself was no option for Masha. Better to live like she did—it was less nerve-wracking.

The eggs finally boiled and Masha put breakfast on the table. The children and her husband chewed unenthusiastically because lately the food tasted terrible for some reason, probably all those chemicals that they were sticking in everything from feed to fertilizer. Masha herself hadn't been able to force any of it down her throat that morning.

Once again she hadn't gotten enough sleep. She dressed hurriedly, grabbing anything that came to hand, and hastily put on her makeup—how can one pick the right shade of eyeshadow this early in the morning! She packed up the older child's bookbag and a little knapsack with a change of shoes and tights for the younger one and ran out of the house. Before work she had to take the children to day care and school. Her husband, mumbling goodbye and not even kissing her, left the house.

At the day-care center and the school Masha listened to the usual complaints about her children's behavior and study habits. But how could they behave and study well, thought Masha in irritation, being left to themselves? They are like street urchins. They had no grandparents, and there was no time to read them smart books and take them around to various activities. God grant that she could at least feed them and put clothes on their backs.

Upset and angry, Masha pushed her way into the packed metro car. She found her nose literally crushed into the back of a young girl wearing a long mink coat down to her heels. She was quite young and rather pretty, although her eyes were completely blank, to the point of transparency. At any rate, even at such an early hour she was very carefully and tastefully made up. The scent of some very fancy, expensive perfume clung to her, probably $80 a bottle or more. In jeans and a short leather jacket, Masha felt like Cinderella, almost a beggar. She had nice things—but just didn't have time to take care of herself, and there was no motivation anyway. Her husband couldn't have cared less whether she wore a brocade dress or a housecoat, and at work they were just a lot of old grumbling women.

Masha once again cast her eyes around the metro car.

Half the women were beautiful and well-dressed, and the closer the train came to the center of Moscow, the more of them boarded. The young women were dressed particularly fashionably—expensive furs despite the early autumn, fancy leather jackets, elegantly stylish boots that Masha had seen costing more than $200 in the store. Where did young girls find money like that? Were they the daughters or lovers of some rich men? Masha grew depressed from her involuntary envy. They couldn't all be secretaries in joint ventures or foreign companies! Perhaps they were just salesgirls making easy money.

Of course she couldn't accuse all of them so groundlessly. Russian women, or rather Soviet women even in the Brezhnev era, were particularly picky about clothes. In the West, professional, wealthy women might go around in old jeans and a ragged sweater and feel great. Here in traditionally poor Soviet Russia, a loader at a vegetable storehouse will pick up rotten potatoes by hand with diamond-ringed fingers, and secretaries staggering from hunger—like characters from the novels of Ludmilla Petrushevskaya—will strut around work in Parisian suits and patent-leather shoes. Now clothes and makeup have somehow taken on a special, almost sacred meaning. They seem to symbolize social status. If one lacks status, one must create the appearance of it. There is a Russian saying that "your clothes get you to the door; your mind gets you through it." Alas, it's your clothes that get you through the door nowadays.

Masha shifted her glance to the perfectly coiffed head of the girl standing in front of her and in embarrassment recalled that she hadn't been near a beauty parlor in three months. There was no time and she felt bad spending the money—in order to get a model's haircut and a perm you needed to throw away half your salary. Still one had to keep up appearances, Masha thought suddenly, and with embarrassment pushed the plastic bag she had brought for groceries deeper into her purse. "The hell with all of it, the kitchen, the housework, the family, and the husband too!" she thought with a sudden surge of hatred. "You have to be free and independent, like that girl over there. You have to love yourself. If you don't love yourself, no one will do it for you." But these were all dreams, only dreams—and Masha knew it. It was a quiet, pointless mutiny. She would still have to take that plastic bag for groceries out of her purse, stuff it to the breaking point, and stagger home with it after work in the crowded metro, like a beast of burden.

Masha glanced at her watch. Lord, it was already 9:30! Late again! That means that she'd be dragged into the personnel department again and have to write an excuse. The department head was already standing in the doorway nabbing latecomers. This was a new trend, the campaign for labor discipline, just as pointless as everything else being done everywhere. Before, the office schedule was fairly relaxed—after all, a proofreader had her quota, and it wasn't important whether you read your hundred pages of manuscript at your desk in the publishing house or at night in your own home. However when the salaries were raised, the bosses decided otherwise. Everyone had to be at their desks, every day, punching a clock. A break could only be taken for lunch. Although there was a pay increase, it was ridiculously low, and life had become unbearable.

Before, when she didn't have to go into work every day, Masha would manage to fit in everything—getting to the store; taking care of the children, dropping them off and picking them up; doing the laundry and housework; and even getting enough sleep. Now the housework had been let go and the apartment was in chaos. Her husband was unhappy, and the children were all but abandoned—and they'd even doubled the quota at work although they paid barely enough to live on. Since more than 50 percent of the payroll was extracted by the state for all sorts of taxes, this was obviously not money but chump change.

The publishing house was churning out all sorts of garbage now—crime stories and romance novels. Only recently, about four years ago, it had been one of the leading publishers in the Soviet Union. Then all the high-class editors were fired—some went over to commercial publishers, some stayed home working freelance. Who wants to sweat for pennies? Now what remained were basically the support staff—the junior editors, the proofreaders, the technical editors—who don't *make* books, but perform services for them: proofing them, cleaning them up, checking for mistakes and typos. Moreover, those who had stayed on for such a ridiculous salary were working unenthusiastically, in a slipshod manner. They mocked their jobs openly as if to say, what, am I going to break my back for that kind of money? One girl remained at half pay in order to keep up a decent face, but earned her real money in a bar as a waitress. She bragged that the other day she had earned $30 in tips—half her monthly salary at the publishing house.

Masha was sick to death of proofing manuscripts, especially the romance novels. She even had suffered a kind of occupational injury from doing this: she had lost the desire to read anything for pleasure now, even good books. The very sight of a printed text nauseated her. Today there was a pile of page proofs on her desk all about the same thing: the happy story of an unhappy but beautiful girl, with whom a rich and noble man falls in love. A new version of the Cinderella story, only with pornographic details. But people love it!

By 2 o'clock the numerous naked breasts started to merge under her mechanical eye into one enormous, round, rose-colored hill, and the bare legs turned into a stack of firewood because Masha was not so much looking for typos as staring at the silent telephone. She was sitting on pins and needles—her daughter should have come home from school a long time ago, but there was still no phone call, and Masha was starting to go quietly out of her mind. How could she remain sane when just the other day a neighbor's child had disappeared in broad daylight on her way home from school, and a maniac had dragged another girl from her daughter's class into the bushes right near the schoolyard and hit her over the head with a bottle?!

Finally the phone rang, and Masha grabbed the receiver. Thank God! She'd gotten through another day. After giving instructions for dinner Masha strictly forbade her daughter to go outside until she got home. Once again she settled down to work. She had to finish reading that garbage as quickly as possible and manage to get to the store in order to buy groceries—and she still had to do some hackwork, a job off the books for another firm, which had promised to pay well for a rush job. She couldn't get along very well on her salary alone.

At last the hand on the clock approached the long-awaited number six. Masha shrugged on her coat and scurried out the door. She had to get to the day-care center quickly to pick up her younger child; otherwise the caregiver would give her a dirty look as she often did—she wanted to get home faster, too. Then Masha had to rush home and take a walk with her daughter and then help her do homework—because her husband, although he was a faithful spouse, was like background decor. Masha had long wondered how to classify her family: a matriarchy or a patriarchy? Recently she suddenly understood that it was a matriarchy at work and a patriarchy at home.

That evening, after washing the dirty dishes left from dinner and putting the children to bed, Masha sat down next to her spouse in front of the television. She gazed dully at the flickering screen, too exhausted even to understand or see what was there. She almost didn't hear what her husband was saying. The evening spell in front of the television set was just a narcotic, a reliable and effective means of shutting off the nastiness and monotony of everyday life and the distasteful anticipation of the night, when her spouse, master, and ruler would call her to come to him.

"I'll get a divorce," thought Masha vengefully through her semi-stupor. "I'll quit! Tomorrow, for sure!" But in her heart of hearts she knew that it was only hysterics; a quiet, pointless mutiny, a rebellion that would be nipped in the bud. By herself. And tomorrow would be the same as today, and the day after that the same as the day before. Then the work week would be over and the hated work weekend would begin with its inevitable huge load of laundry, ironing, cleaning, and the long, happy stroll of the happy family.

The newspapers and television never tire of assuring us that there's a boom in Russian brides now. Foreign husbands are running in droves to marry Russian women.

Even if this is partially true, I don't think it is because Russian women are so pretty. It is mainly because even a very attractive, intelligent, and educated Russian woman usually is completely devoid of something her foreign, particularly her Western, counterpart possesses—an awareness of her own significance, or to put it cynically, of her price. Russian women are raised this way—and always have been, both before and after the revolution. They have grown used to sacrificing themselves willingly, with alacrity, submerging themselves into husband, family, and country.

In the mid-seventeenth century, noble and wealthy women in Russia lived as virtual prisoners under the all-watchful eyes of first their parents and then their husbands. They were forbidden to leave the house or to sit at the same table with men, much less have any fun. When a spouse found it convenient to introduce his wife to his guests, she did not dare even to speak. This subservience in us came from Asia, after the Mongolian-Tatar Yoke, under Tsar Ivan III. (In ancient Rus women were free and equal with men.) Ever since this time Russia has been a kind of odd, contradictory hybrid of West and East, above all in the area of the family.

Made greedy by the constant lack of money and raised in an atmosphere of universal parasitism and egalitarianism, the Russian man is unable and even unwilling to take responsibility for a woman. He magnanimously allows her to earn a living, raise the children, take care of him—the spouse and lord—and to arrange and beautify everyday life. He himself does not lower himself to such trivialities. Thus are the overwhelming majority of Soviet, and now post-Soviet, men constructed.

Among plainer folk the man quite often drinks up his pay; in families that are more sophisticated the husband on principle does not give his pay to his family, keeping it to himself for his "incidental expenses." Public morality never condemns licentious behavior by men, although it does not approve of women's illicit lovelives.

In Russia men actually fear beauty, talent, and intelligence in a woman. Some of my male acquaintances admit to me that they fear independent women like the devil. As for women who decide to make a professional or artistic career, their chances of a happy family life are almost nil—Russian men will not tolerate such competition! My own divorce happened precisely for this reason, and in fact all my subsequent romances ended rather sadly—no one tolerates a girlfriend who is too involved in creative work.

Even the most cultured of men simply prefer to have as a wife a servant, a private secretary, and a mother for their children, with whom it is possible to preserve complete personal freedom of movement. I recall the movie star Fateyeva, whose first husband was a famous and very talented film director. Many years after the divorce she complained in an interview that he had literally driven her mad with the remark, "I wish you would get old faster!" Former Russian presidential advisor Galina Starovoitova once let slip the price of her career: "I was able to make something of myself at a great cost—the ruin of my health, the loss of my family, the renunciation of my creativity."[12]

Paradoxically, the most ordinary women have the happiest family lives because they have no special ambitions and do not irritate their husbands with beauty and talent. It is very curious to observe the recent tendency in the families of the newly rich to return to a complete patriarchy. The wife in such a family is virtually reduced to a slave: her husband forbids her to work and almost never takes her with him to a restaurant, to the theater, or to visit other people. If he brings home people who are important to him, his wife is obliged to serve dinner silently without entering into business conversations. Toward the end of the evening the men are usually drunk and go off to have a good time in the nightclubs, leaving their wives to gossip and smoke nervously, bored until morning. Can they call their husbands at the office? Out of the question. Their husbands would be very unhappy with that. Moreover they are forced to reconcile themselves to the existence of their husbands' almost legitimized mistresses. All that is left these rich but unhappy women is to raise their children (strictly supervised by their husbands) and keep themselves up—go to the beauty parlor, the sauna, and the cosmetic salons in the company of other such victims of sudden wealth.

Obviously, taking care of your beauty doesn't bring you much pleasure if your husband isn't spending the night at home. Among the many women who call the confidential hotlines of the emergency mental health services are the unhappy wives of our new businessmen who have come upon wealth, and usually they're calling about family problems.

Of course there are families in Russia where mutual respect, love, and equality prevail—but these are rather the exception than the rule. As for feminism, we can only dream of it. Although there are women who call themselves feminists in Russia, and even a feminist conference circuit, in such an economically backward country, progressive movements have a hard time getting off the ground. For feminism to become a reality of daily life as it is in America, women first must be freed from their domestic burdens and then given professional opportunities equal to those of men. As long as women live like Masha it is futile to even talk of equality.

The equality of the sexes proclaimed after the October Revolution basically amounted to women in Russia gaining the right to dig ditches and haul rails alongside men. They were not admitted into the highest posts of the government, much less into diplomatic careers, and it is only recently that women have been allowed into the army. Under the economic reforms the status of women—both economic and social—has fallen disastrously. Women are the first to be fired and make up most of the unemployed. In industry the number of women managers is tiny, and it's the same sad story in the government. The few women in these areas are barely distinguishable from men. I only know of two examples in Russia where public or government activity is successfully combined with beauty and charm, without damaging femininity: Irina Khakamada, a deputy of the State Duma, a rare, brilliant and effective woman; and Ella Pamfilova, a very charming former minister of social security.

Recently I have noticed a strange tendency among women of all sectors of society from the intelligentsia to the working class: they are increasingly and voluntarily willing to deny themselves equality; they are increasingly willing to sit at home and leave their jobs. If ten years ago it was considered shameful to be a housewife, now no one is bothered by such a notion. This could be expressed in even stronger terms: women no longer want equality; they are tired of the Soviet-style equality of the workplace. They can no longer overstrain themselves in this way, and therefore are only too glad to choose voluntary slavery of any variety —in the role of wife, or lover, or kept woman. They do not oppose the return to the patriarchy—as long as the men are responsible for them and their children. And this is at the end of the twentieth century!

Journalist Alexander Terekhov published an article
in the March 1991 issue of the magazine *Ogonyok* that aptly
summarizes the Russian woman's lot:

> Why do our women burn out so quickly, mobi-
> lized and crushed by the sexless and harsh times
> of our national battles? Why is there no other age
> except "girl" and "granny"? Why does beauty toil
> for foreign currency for export, and intelligence,
> unhappy and lonely, vegetate in boring parlia-
> mentary meetings in a male suit jacket or bang
> her fist on the podium in constant hysteria? Why
> have decent beauty and attractive intelligence be-
> come lost somewhere in the last centuries, and the
> few crumbs that remain been lured abroad with
> promises of the good life, long-lasting beauty, a
> secure old age, and unlimited choice, and not
> merely of which line to stand in? Why is it that
> in the neglected villages the last folk songs are
> preserved by the ancient old ladies, with no one
> to take their place? Our women are disappearing
> somewhere. Why are there so very few of them?[13]

More than four years have passed since this article
appeared—an eternity, full of dramatic events. Those who
had a choice in those years made use of their chance. Whoever did not fall into the abyss of poverty and misfortune,
whoever did not sink up to her neck in the quagmire of
everyday life, dirty dishes, and diapers, whoever grabbed her
lucky chance has set sail. But now there are only two—

alas!—two types of occupations that can keep you afloat: so-called love and so-called business.

∿

For decades Communist propaganda claimed that prostitution did not exist in the USSR. If there was no problem, that meant there was no research or statistics, and since there was no research or statistics, it seemed that the problem didn't exist, either—that was the vicious circle. But those who lived in the old days remember and testify that there was such a problem, not only in the Khrushchev and Brezhnev eras, but even in the brutal years of the Stalin regime. In fact prostitutes were not so harshly punished: in the criminal code, which has been preserved in virtually unchanged form since the revolution, there is not even an article specifically punishing prostitutes—only pimps and keepers of brothels. Back in the years of the New Economic Plan (NEP) in the 1920s, prostitutes gained all their civil rights, making them equal to the rest of citizens. If any measures were taken to curb prostitutes (for example, during Khrushchev's day, they were often deported from Moscow beyond the 101st kilometer), the basis for the punishment was usually a charge like "habitual parasitism."

Vladimir Kunin's book *Intergirl* (a play on the phrase "international girl") broke the wall of silence on the subject in 1988 and was soon made into a movie, signaling the triumphant rise of the Soviet prostitute to the height of honor and fame. Her time had come, and songs and films were now being dedicated to her. The Russian idea of the beautiful woman, the "mysterious lady" once lauded by the wonderfully subtle poet Alexander Blok, evolved rapidly during the years of Gorbachev's and Yeltsin's rule as a new type of beauty, embodied in the prostitute, found recognition.

After the victory over the August coup, Russian prostitution entered a new period: the dizzying ascent of the "night butterfly," who hitherto had tried to remain in the shadows. Though the country's newly acquired "freedom" was often an illusion, it was enough to allow prostitution, still not legalized, to flourish abundantly. Moscow's first whorehouse was quickly followed by others, multiplying like mushrooms after a summer rain. Newspapers began to run ads luring clients into the chambers of love. There was only one restriction: the men had to be well-to-do. "Tender and charming girls from the firm Annushka will spend an unforgettable evening with well-to-do gentlemen," reads one ad. "Two (or one) young, charming, bisexual girls, nice to be with, will spend an evening with very well-off gentlemen." "Gentlemen! Just say your wish and our golden fish will hurry to fulfill it any time of day or night. Our possibilities are unlimited! From lesbie shows to the impossible."

Prostitutes don't have to freeze outside on the streets anymore to attract clients. A "dispatcher" from such a "firm" sits in an apartment especially rented for the purpose and takes orders by telephone. A bodyguard takes the girl to the necessary address and settles the payment. Ever since the authorities began cracking down on newspapers for procuring, the advertisers have changed their tactics. Now they don't offer "erotic massages," but "dinner and drinks with escort" and mysterious "companion services"—and everyone gets the message.

Sometimes the owners of such services (which, incidentally, change their dispatchers' addresses and telephone numbers so often it is impossible to catch them) are former

Komsomol workers who were famous for their degraded morals even in the Soviet era. The clients of such escort services are the usual tired businessmen, majors, bohemians, and foreign travelers. It is said that there is even a subscription plan now so that entire organizations can enjoy the services of a firm's "girls." The situation is very reminiscent of the days of the NEP, when hunger, expensive goods, the appearance of a class of merchants, and as a consequence, the increase in the demand for "live wares," led to similar results.

The differentiation of prostitutes into classes began under Gorbachev. The elite *putana* (from the French *putain*), or intergirls, worked for foreign currency and exclusively with foreigners. Many had higher degrees and the ability to speak foreign languages. The ordinary prostitutes worked for rubles, preferably with sailors whose voyages took them abroad, northerners on vacation, and military officers who traveled to the city on business. The "lower-class" prostitutes got along however they could, accompanying long-haul drivers of refrigerated trucks on intercity routes, for example. For that reason, they were nicknamed "highway women." Sometimes they solicited in train stations, performing sexual acts right on the floor in deserted station hallways or toilets, perhaps for some cheap wine or a piece of bread.

As in the old days, today's prostitutes have preserved their elite and have their "dregs." But in comparison with the Gorbachev period, prostitutes in Russia have become drastically younger, and many suffer from syphilis. Little girls start selling their bodies at the age of ten or eleven, sometimes at a rock-bottom price. Oral sex or intercourse in a car, doorway, or basement is given for only $2 or $3. That is barely enough money to have lunch at McDonalds, but it's freedom. In the brothels, of course, sex with minors comes at a far higher price, and it's a real prison from which the children can never escape. For young girls from poor families, especially where the parents are alcoholics, prostitution is the only chance to get to the beautiful life. However, quite a few nymphets from well-to-do families stumble onto the path of depravity—not surprising for a society whose national ideal of a woman is not Natasha Rostova (the long-admired heroine of *War and Peace*) but a hard-currency prostitute.

The other day there was a new movie on television called *Dating Service*. Four women—a bartender, an art historian, an unemployed girl, and even the wife of a minister—were making money on the side as call girls for the mighty of this world. They were beautiful, chic, and stylishly made up, with wads of rubles and dollars. Why had these women chosen this path? All of them—including the minister's wife—said that they wanted to secure their future and the future of their family. During the movie the girls almost died at the hands of gangsters, but in the end everyone was happy. They were saved either by the OMON (the police riot troops) or the Alpha special division (who took part in suppressing both the August coup and the October rebellion); the girls' powerful patrons even had the State Security Service at their beck and call. Justice triumphed and the "oldest profession" probably got some new recruits from the audience.

Those who wish to sell their bodies now have a wide variety of opportunities. If you like, you can become a "bull girl", i.e., a girl who services gangsters, an item of exchange and bargaining, a thing, a bed accessory, who is paid not even in cash, but in the illusion of the good life with clothes, restaurants, rides in fancy automobiles, radios, and videos.

Or you can go into modeling, and if you want to work your way up and travel abroad, you can sleep with everything in pants in your company or give them 30 percent of your hard-currency profits—that is, if you want to work your way up. If you're lucky, maybe you can land yourself a financial "sponsor," which is what rich lovers and patrons are now cynically called in Russia. Or you can chose an even more unusual route—becoming a dancer at a "foreign cabaret" (read: whorehouse). For a price, some theaters in Moscow are happy to give aspiring visa-seekers a diploma as a professional dancer within five days.

Actually, in order to sell yourself it's not necessary to go to these extremes. Pretty girls with long legs, especially blondes, may sell themselves quite simply and profitably. Career-related prostitution on the job has been quite common from the earliest years of Soviet rule when there appeared a needy class of women called "Soviet ladies"—semidestitute secretaries, typists, telephone operators, and so on. Now it's not so easy to get a job as a secretary in a commercial firm. You need either connections or a pretty face and figure. It's no secret what your *job* will be there, apart from your stated duties. It often happens that Russian firms (and even foreign companies) hire two or even three girls for one job—one "work horse" who will carry the whole workload and two for sexual favors. It is a very wide-spread practice and no one is surprised or outraged—as if that's the way things should be. On the contrary, people are surprised or even condescendingly amused when in America or Europe the usual scandal breaks out over the sexual so-licitation by some political boss. "Those American and European girls are too independent," people say. And really, we should have such problems! We've got enough of our own in Russia. It's a free market now. Anybody can sell anything. Even the creative types—the previously popular and very independent actresses, artists, television anchorwomen—are eagerly looking for rich men to keep them, and are becoming the objects of gutter newspaper gossip.

In general these women are not to blame. Indeed the Soviet government was right to give prostitutes equal rights with other citizens. But unquestionably, society and the state are to blame for the fact that prostitutes now live better than ordinary women. A woman has only one life to live and it is so short; she wants to live it in beauty, despite all the reforms and perestroikas. Even if the price of such "beauty" is so high.

It's sad, very sad, that Russian women are so willing to sell themselves now—when there are buyers and when there is a reason to sell—and it is sadder still to see so many women used for nothing, like objects, and with such cynicism. But those who have taken this slippery slope did not do so because of some basic flaw in the Russian female nature, or at least, not all of them. Their country, their Motherland—along with its men—pushed them to the edge of this precipice.

∾

What about free love outside of marriage? What novelties have perestroika and economic reform brought to this area? People fooled around on the side and cheated on their husbands and wives in the old days, of course. But it was done in secret, cautiously, since open and provocative debauchery could lead to dismissal from work, expulsion from the Party, destruction of one's career, and a general

scandal—at a minimum, an administrative or Party repri-
mand on one's record.

Russia's sexual boom is now splashed all over the
pages of newspapers and magazines. The most intimate details are discussed openly, with relish—things that the closest
of girlfriends were too embarrassed to tell each other even a
year or two ago. An example:

> I am twenty-one years old. I am an affectionate
> blonde with green eyes. I dream of meeting a per-
> son I could call My Man. I'm ready to be under-
> standing and forgive brief liaisons but in the long
> run he should be Mine. I want to be only with
> him day in and day out, and to make new dis-
> coveries in our relations every day. I dream of
> walking around the apartment only in my bath-
> robe, so that he can always reach his hand under.
> . . . Or if I'm busy, I'd like him to sneak up
> behind me, put his hands through the opening,
> and caress my breasts (and there is plenty to touch
> there). Or if I'm washing my underwear in the
> bathtub, and he comes in, he tears off my robe
> and takes possession of me.[14]

This epistolic masterpiece (virtually the most chaste
in this thick journal of personals) ends with a passionate plea:
"I am willing and able to be your mistress and servant! I
really want to! But only with one man." (Others want much
more—two men or even a whole group.)

Sometimes I am dumbfounded; these are just young
girls, after all. And they aren't ashamed of writing things
like that about themselves in the newspapers, and even put-

ting in their addresses and telephone numbers? Does this
represent dissipation, a collapse of morals comparable to the
fall of the Roman Empire? Or is it just dense stupidity, feeding on the pornography that our publishing houses are now
churning out so avidly? I don't know. What is sadder is how
this girl imagines the joys of sex—while cleaning the apartment, standing at the kitchen stove, washing her underwear
in the bathtub. This unhappy little Russian fool—her whole
life watching her mother ground down by work and everyday chores—couldn't possibly imagine anything else!

Here is another pearl, a real psychological masterpiece:

> My friends often call me Honey—for my sweet-
> ness, probably. I'm twenty-one years old and a
> college student. Moscow is my drug. I love
> women and I'm happy with myself and my ability
> to love. When I read letters from forty-year-old
> women who have come to the late realization that
> they are lesbians, and who have never tried female
> love, I'm saddened. I'm a real gift (I'm certain of
> it) for ladies thirty-five to forty-five. Single or
> married, but lesbians at heart. It's important for
> you to be a Muscovite and to have an apartment
> for rendezvous. If you want, I can be your daugh-
> ter and lover simultaneously. Conversation is im-
> portant. I am serious about literature and can
> understand the Soul of a Woman better than Bal-
> zac. I will not just heal your body, I will heal
> your soul above all!!! I will heal your wounds,
> anointing them with the balm of Eastern philos-
> ophy. I am dreaming so of bringing you calm and

happiness! I am waiting for your letter but you must value your individuality for I, too, cannot waste myself in vain. What's important is not the external, but your inner being. I cannot imagine such a nature among factory workers, train conductors, accountants, etc. If you are involved in art or in creative work then we are kindred souls. . . .[15]

There's no point in quoting this further. The image of a young, provincial predator trying to sell herself to a Muscovite with a coveted apartment is already fairly stark.

Where is the world headed? And where has Russia gone? I understand the men and women who have seized upon free sex after so many years of the strictest taboos and hypocritical social morality, and the groups who have wrested a recognition of their rights from the authorities at long last. But many have simply lost themselves in an alien world, and are trying to grasp at straws.

Chapter 9

Save Our Souls

The mortal body is easy to subordinate; a whole range of often-tried methods exist to move the human form humbly to the place where Power pushes it. The soul is another matter; ethereal and elusive, it cannot be captured by steel traps and coarse nooses. Special lures are needed, as silken and soft as the soul itself. The soul is susceptible and trusting: if you stroke it the right way and say a kind word, like a cat it will jump up on your lap.

The Russian soul has a peculiar construction: it needs a tsar or a god, or at least an idol, and an antichrist. It cannot remain independent on its own, and live by rational laws; it cannot be a full vessel unless filled with a mystical, pure faith.

The revolution took faith in Christ away from us and in return gave us a new god (Marxism-Leninism) and new priests (the great leaders of Communism). In time the priests themselves became gods. The new faith didn't particularly stand on ceremony with delicate souls, driving them with a lash into a narrow corral. But the souls, knowing no other master, were obedient and did not resist—with the exception of a few renegade sheep who spoiled the flock.

In August 1991 the cathedral of this faith collapsed. Now the Communist regime, like a hydra with its head cut off, lies in a puddle of fetid blood, and the orphaned souls are stamping confusedly at the collapsing walls of the corral not knowing where to go, trembling in the piercing wind of uncomfortable freedom.

Everyone thought the once-reviled flower of Christianity would flourish in vibrant and profuse color, bringing enlightenment and purification to a people defiled by sin. Unfortunately, however, this has not yet happened. Most likely quite a bit of time and desire will be needed for a new flower to grow.

∾

It is no secret that the official church, although separate from the state, cooperated with the Soviet regime. Documents discovered in the archives confirm that its highest clergy worked hand in glove with the agencies of oppression, supplying information to the KGB (although there were also decent priests who declared the Soviet government anathema, for which they ended their lives in labor camps and prisons.)

In those years only those who ran no risk of losing a bureaucratic post or ruining a career could get married or baptized in churches without looking over their shoulders. Those who were even slightly higher than the ordinary working stiff would not dare to make such an open demonstration of their scorn of the existing unwritten prohibitions, especially those in the sphere of ideology—the cultural and information/propaganda institutions including publishing houses and the media.

I myself came to God rather late, when I was already thirty years old. It was a difficult period in my life, when it seemed that all hope and faith in myself and other people were lost. I realized that without faith in God I would simply not survive, and decided to be baptized. Even at that time when perestroika was in full swing, I had to hunt through acquaintances for a priest who would perform the ritual in secret without registering my passport information in the parish book—otherwise I would have been fired from my publishing job within a week.

When Abuladze's famous film *Repentance* came out in 1986, there was a sudden burgeoning of spirituality, especially among the intelligentsia. People sincerely believed in renewal, in the possibility of purification from filth, and realized that if the road did not lead to the cathedral of faith, then it went nowhere.* The politicians also realized this, in their own way, of course. A new trend took off—a merging of government authority with the official church, under the sign of unity of the cross and the red star. The powers-that-be began to appear before the television cameras at church services, holding candles in rigid hands and clumsily crossing themselves. The church meanwhile concerned itself with getting back the property the state had seized from it in the 1920s.

The authorities today need the church—the official

* In the last scene of *Repentance*, a man asks an old woman, "Is this the road that leads to the cathedral?" She replies, "And what kind of road is it, if it doesn't lead to the cathedral?"—Trans.

church—even more than they did under Communism. Christ has suddenly become necessary to strengthen political power. That is why everybody—the "democrats," the opposition, the fascists, and the "national-patriots"—now flock to church. Already betrayed and crucified once, Christ is now being used by people who push and elbow each other out of the way in their haste to tear pieces of his shroud and attach them as flags to various ideas and doctrines—starting with the idea of the great power, the special role of Russia, "Orthodoxy," and imperial politics, and ending with fascism, Nazism and anti-Semitism.

The churches now are packed with parishioners during services. It is unthinkable today not to marry or baptize a child in church. At Eastertime, the lines of people wishing to bless their traditional holiday *kulich* (sweet bread) and eggs stretch on and on, winding in circles around the churches. People also stand for hours so that a drop of holy water might touch them. In what do they believe with such fervor?

A great many of them are true believers regardless of what position the official church takes. They are people striving to believe in good and live by God's law. There are even priests, real zealots, who bring light and faith to people, not only in the churches, but in prisons, labor colonies, and in the army. I met such people—they have radiant eyes and open faces—when my daughter attended Sunday school.

But it is so easy to substitute faith, true faith, with false belief, and God with a fraud and an idol. The Russian people have been separated from God for so long that at times they have forgotten how to distinguish good from evil. Some of the people filling the cathedrals now—headed by political leaders—believe in nothing at all. For them this is just the latest fashion, a sign of their respectability. For others it is part of a necessary ritual serving to reinforce their political image and their struggle for power.

There are also some who visit the churches who do believe, but often not in what the Bible teaches. In his novel *Silence*, the Japanese Catholic writer Shusaku Endo explores the reasons for the failure of Christianity in medieval Japan. One of the novel's protagonists, a Portuguese missionary apostate, says:

> In the churches we built throughout this country the Japanese were not praying to the Christian God. They twisted God to their own way of thinking in a way we can never imagine. . . . That is not God. It is like a butterfly caught in a spider's web. At first it is certainly a butterfly, but the next day only the externals, the wings and the trunk, are those of a butterfly; it has lost its true reality and has become a skeleton.[16]

The Bolsheviks, once they had caught the butterfly of the church in their nets, did the same thing with Jesus. Therefore it is now most important to return the true God to people—but how? Certainly not by decrees from on high.

Recently it was decided to restore to its previous condition Moscow's Church of Christ the Savior, which Stalin had ordered dynamited. Will that really purify our souls? Whenever Empress Catherine II traveled, artificial villages were constructed along the road on orders of her favorite, Prince Potemkin, in order to delight the monarch's eye. In the Brezhnev era, whenever high-ranking guests came from abroad, the lawns were spraypainted green. Now they will erect the Christian cathedrals again? Even people who simply believe in God have their doubts. I recall a letter to the editor in a newspaper:

> The construction of fake cathedrals is not repentance, but merely a whitewashing of sins. The symbol of the destroyed cathedral is a brand of shame against a disgustingly inhumane system. So in the name of what are they trying to wipe away this brand of shame? It turns out to be in the name of "new great-power thinking." But is there a borderline in Russia between great-power and imperial thinking? And what difference does it make what is built in the name of a great power—a cathedral or a Palace of Soviets?[17]

In order to renew Russia, severely sickened with faithlessness, cynicism, and brutality, we really do need a cathedral. Not just a church erected from bricks and steel, but a cathedral of the soul—the Cathedral of True Faith.

∾

A holy place does not remain vacant for long. So goes the Russian proverb. The place left in people's souls from the ruined Orthodox faith did not remain empty. Hands were outstretched from the other side of the river to the orphaned souls. The first to be taken were those weak in spirit, who had lost their way in the coming apocalyptic gloom.

Sects existed in Russia even in the old days, although the church banned them as heretics before the October Revolution. After the revolution, the state outlawed them. Now that everything is permissible, sects are flourishing in the Russian spiritual desert. There are quite a few new ones; some are harmless but others, known as "totalitarian sects," bring people evil and suffering under the guise of enlightenment and purification.

There are about two hundred totalitarian sects in Russia (some of whose activities fall under the criminal code), including groups such as Aum Shinrikyo (founded by the Japanese preacher, Shoko Asahara), the Virgin Center, the infamous White Brotherhood (now banned), the Krishna Society for Religious Consciousness, Rev. Moon's Unification Church, Tantrists, neo-Satanists, Mormons, and also groups like the New Apostolic Church, the Church of Christ, and so on.

Many sects are notable for their furious recruitment of new members, their large number of followers, and their powerful support from abroad. Such churches often feature a hierarchical system, a cult of the Teacher, and semi-military discipline. As for the teachings themselves, as a rule they are eclectic and syncretic in nature—a mixture of the most diverse religious doctrines. The terms for membership in these sects are usually harsh, sometimes even requiring them to sever relations with families, leave home, and donate their personal and household property to the sect.

Many young people join the totalitarian sects, particularly those with higher degrees, people inclined toward mysticism and fascinated with esoteric teachings, and some who feel they are failures in life. They come to the sect in search of reassurance or thrills, and it offers them the surrogate of a full life in the form of religious ecstasy. Some are sincerely searching for salvation, something the Russian Orthodox Church was unable to provide. Some, it seems, are all too ready to be fooled. As the newspaper *Segodnya* (To-day) commented, "When someone comes along promising a quick fix and a recipe for universal salvation (without particular effort on the part of those saved), people will follow him, regardless of who he is—Zhirinovshky, Mavrodi, or Asahara. This is a feature of the Russian mentality, but it is also the basis of totalitarianism."[18]

The totalitarian sects use a wide range of bizarre methods to win impressionable converts. Some employ rites of initiation that include mass rallies, hypnosis, fasts, sleep deprivation, special diets, meditation, and group chanting of mantras to induce a trance-like state. Indeed a few groups, like Aum Shinrikyo, have been accused of using mechanical devices (such as helmets that emit ultrasound waves) to further their control. The results are staggering: sometimes literally within the space of a few days people who had previously ridiculed a sect become its fiercest devotees.

I have long wanted to see what these sects were like from within and to understand how people's relations are established in such sects and what their daily life is like. It is easy to get into a sect, but penetrating its inner core is extremely difficult for a rank-and-file member—and it didn't make sense for me to start from the ground up and spend years getting brainwashed. Then I had an unexpected stroke of luck: a friend invited me to visit the Hare Krishnas for the "partaking of the delicacies," or, to put it in everyday language, to visit the highest leaders of the society!

The Krishna Society for Religious Consciousness (they categorically refuse to call themselves a sect) occupies a fairly large and quite comfortable building of twenty-eight rooms, brimming with modern and very expensive telecommunications and video equipment. About thirty people live there—the devoted initiates, apparently those especially close to the leadership and those who serve in the office. Downstairs is a prayer hall with an altar for visiting believers. There are three prayer services a day and three partakings of the delicacies. They also have their own farm, radio program, and publishing house. They put out books and give interviews like the most seasoned of television stars. There is an impression of extreme respectability and affluence—and no wonder. As I understood it, the donations (mainly from India) are pouring in.

Until the late 1980s the Hare Krishnas, who opposed the Soviet regime, were harshly punished under the criminal code for "refusal to perform socially useful work" or engaging in religious practices "damaging to health" and forced to serve in the army. The founders of the sect had their fill of Soviet prisons but did not abandon their ideas. But now that the problem with the authorities is over and the sect has won official recognition, they have suddenly retreated on some issues. For example sect members are now allowed to serve in the army, despite the Society's ban on killing living creatures.

"How can that be?" I asked in surprise.

"A person can kill an aggressor," they replied.

"But how can you determine who is the aggressor in the inter-ethnic conflicts?" I asked, puzzled.

"You have to think with your head," the chief ideologue of the sect answered evasively. "But generally our members serve in the army construction crews. The army commanders allow them to perform their bathing rituals and not eat meat."

That's curious, I thought. You're not allowed to eat meat, but you can kill people.

I was not very interested in the sect's teachings—
especially since they were expounded in a very vague form
—and so I quickly tried to turn the conversation from the
exalted and theoretical track to something more earthbound,
particularly the daily practices of the Society. It turned out
that the Hare Krishnas' daily routine, aside from their services (prayer sessions), amounted to the following: communal
chanting, festival street processions, charitable work (handing
out free food), translation of religious literature, publication
of books, and performance of concerts and lectures. Given
the presence of the farm, commerce was obviously another
activity.

The Society's elite consisted of members of the
intelligentsia—musicians, artists, and actors. Some people
had left their families for the sake of the sect and sacrificed
their belongings. The spiritual teacher was from India. The
ideologue, a former Moscow State University student from
the department of psychology, was a particularly intriguing
figure to me, articulate and knowledgeable. I fell into an
interesting conversation with him. When I complained that
innocent children suffered from the activities of some sects
when they were separated from their parents, he replied
sternly that "in general there are no innocent lambs, since
under the law of Karma, a person is sinful from the beginning because he bears the burden of the sins of his previous
incarnations. And in general only he who wants to be deceived is deceived—and those children who join such sects
get a sinful pleasure from their sense of being chosen."

While we were talking with the leadership and tour-
ing the house, barefoot young men and women were dashing
about, watchful and tense. They shot guarded looks at the
outsiders, as if they were protecting their teachers and stood

ready to come at their first beck and call. As I found out later from other sources, those who live at the sect permanently are mainly adolescents from troubled families—children of alcoholics, prostitutes, and the homeless; in a word, those rejected and cast out by life. The zeal of service burned in their eyes. The barrier between themselves—the youngest pupils—and the leadership, despite the outwardly democratic relations, was almost palpable.

When I left, a service was just beginning in the prayer hall. Many young people had gathered, well-dressed people, including couples with small children. It was obvious that these were prosperous members of the intelligentsia.

"What, in fact, is the purpose of the Society?" I asked in parting.

"The golden age will come in seventy thousand years. But now is the era of hypocrisy, lies, and degradation. We, the Hare Krishnas, with our spiritual activity, are helping to bring about a change in the unfavorable course of history. For example the nuclear war predicted by Nostradamus did not happen only thanks to us, although up until 1965 all his predictions were coming true!" they told me.

Although on the whole the Hare Krishnas made a favorable impression on me, I sensed the kind of magnetic attraction for young people—for those who do not accept the current reality—hidden within the closed selectivity of such a caste organization. Nevertheless neither their activities nor their teachings provoked a sense of protest and I thought, better social activity and festival processions than crime and prostitution. In its own way the Society was a form of fighting evil, at the contemporary stage. At least they did not, like some sects, teach people to leave their families, bow down to evil and the antichrist, or issue apocalyptic calls for mass suicide. For example the hysteria around the White

Brotherhood (also known as Jusmalos, which means "the right of evil") nearly ended in tragedy when its living god, Devi Maria Christ, announced the coming end of the world. Almost 80,000 hypnotized people, mainly adolescents, began to gather at the Cathedral of Saint Sophia in Kiev. Why? They had been promised a "mass assumption into heaven."

I even know a family who lost their daughter to a sect. First, the mother began to notice peculiar things about her daughter's behavior—a wandering gaze, strange phrases. Then the girl unleashed a flood of hatred on her mother, calling her a witch and "the devil's offspring." Finally she packed her bags, took some money, and left. Forever. To the other side of the river. To the sect called the Virgin Center who preach that people have only one real mother, the Mother of God, and that their natural mothers are a creation of the devil. My acquaintances were a fairly successful family and no one could explain why such a breakdown would occur in such a well-loved child. They were not able to get the girl back, despite all attempts by the police. The sect hid her away in a clandestine apartment. Souls rarely return from the other side of the river.

∾

Modern Russia is reminiscent in some ways of Germany after World War I, when occultism and astrology flourished and magic reigned, whipping up the hysteria that fostered the development of Nazism. Interest in mysticism is always piqued by tragic turning points in history, but there have never been so many people involved with the occult sciences and paranormal phenomena in Russia as there are now.

Two years ago the evidence of this was only bubbling

on the surface like foam, but now it has penetrated throughout everyday life. Wherever you look on television or in the
newspapers, astrologists and magicians, shamans and traditional psychics, warlocks and witches, healers and medicine
men, seers and clairvoyants, and channelers who contact ex-
traterrestrial civilizations are all making predictions for politicians and offering their services to the public. For a rather
handsome sum you can have your horoscope read, find a
missing relative using a photograph, get back a husband who
has left you for a mistress (or the opposite, put a spell on
your lover to get him to leave his wife), get rid of the evil
eye or put a deadly hex on someone, foretell the future or
change your karma, cure alcoholism, cast a magic spell, heal
yourself of physical and spiritual ailments, or jinx your enemies and competitors. There are numerous schools, courses,
and academies of all types where you can learn these crafts
yourself, where there are courses in telling fortunes by the
stars, healing, casting spells, and harnessing or simply invok-
ing the forces of darkness or cosmic energy.

I was particularly intrigued by a school of witches
that opened in Moscow and is now accepting beautiful
women as students. The purpose of the course is to help
businessmen with difficult negotiations by having witches
cast spells on their clients. The methods taught are psycho-
analysis, hypnosis, extrasensory perception, herbal cures,
fortune-telling with cards, interpretation of dreams, control
of poltergeists, and clairvoyance. You can also program people for success. True, the tuition is $5,000 for a year-long
course but, as the director of the school says, the certified
witch will see a full return of this fee in profits two months
after she begins practicing. Upon graduation she will receive
a diploma certifying that she is a witch! Very tempting.

Another curious ad:

The first school of occultism in Russia:
meditation of the Silver Fairy Maria de Elfana.
Also lectures on contact with higher Spiritual
Forces; unique methods of cosmic healing and re-
moval of spells (during the lectures clairvoyance
and telepathic contact will be discovered, and supernatural abilities revealed); tarot cards and nu-
merology; Tibetan medicine; medical astrology;
astral music; reading of karma.

In order to acquire supernatural knowledge, you don't
even have to put yourself out and go to lectures—it's enough
to watch television regularly and read the newspapers and
magazines. They're all publishing tons of useful knowledge.

Do you know, for example, how to put a spell on
your lover? Put his photograph on your left knee, face down.
Write his name on it and read an incantation, then burn it,
open the window, and scatter the ashes to the wind at mid-
night, when the cosmic information channels are open. Or just
hex some salt or wine and give it to him. To remove a spell on
the other hand, cross yourself with a knife and then run it
through a flame. If you would like to put someone to death,
just knead a little figure out of wax, pierce it with a knitting
needle or a pin, and then throw it in a fire. And so forth and
so on. These are the kind of helpful hints you can find in the
Russian media these days—and I'm not speaking of the tab-
loids, but the quite respectable newspapers and magazines.

In the past only the most select, the most worthy,
were initiated into mystical secrets. Now the doors of mystery have swung open for all comers—for the pure of heart
and the selfish, for those striving toward light and those
wishing to serve darkness. Just put down your cold hard
cash.

The times have passed when everyone was amused at political skirmishes in which supporters of the president and supporters of the parliament each brought in psychics to sit with them so that they could conduct their invisible wars. No one is laughing because it has become all too serious. Yes, the art of government is a great temptation. This trial is hard to overcome. Perhaps that is why the government, including the security service and the Ministry of Defense, has turned a blind eye to the sects. Indeed, these groups are given easy access to the best civic arenas and stadiums, as well as to government-controlled mass media outlets.

For several years now, the faith healers Kashpirovsky and Chumak have performed their feats on millions of people, while the authorities have benignly looked on. The theories of L. Ron Hubbard are put into practice at factories employing tens of thousands of workers, and training sessions using his techniques have been run for the heads of regional legislatures and mayors of large cities. Even the infamous Japanese sect Aum Shinrikyo has found favor with the authorities. The cult's leaders met with top government officials, including chief security advisor Oleg Lobov, who are believed to have encouraged the group; their experimentation with chemicals apparently attracted the interest of Russia's secret police. Indeed, when Japanese police raided Aum Shinrikyo after the March 1995 gas attacks in the Tokyo subway, the cult was discovered to possess a Russian-made military helicopter and gas analyzers that are manufactured at a top-secret laboratory in Moscow.

This type of activity is unprecedented in Russia. Did we really not have enough of being zombies for seventy years under Communist rule? It seems we are still a nation of obedient guinea pigs, although now in a spiritual laboratory.

Chapter 10

Permanent Shock

At one time Russia was threatened by only one terrible ghost haunting Europe—the "specter of Communism." In recent years the number of phantoms has grown tremendously. They now haunt Russia in droves, and the feeling of constant amazement that seized us early in the year has long since turned into a permanent, persistent shock.

The December 1993 parliamentary elections thoroughly spoiled our New Year's joy. In both election-by-party lists, and direct district elections for the State Duma, Zhirinovsky's party—the Liberal-Democratic Party of Russia—did far better than even the government-backed Russia's Choice. Except for the sparsely populated districts of the far North, out of our whole enormous country, only the democratic oases of the big metropolitan centers—Moscow, St. Petersburg, the Ural Mountain cities, and Khabarovsk—were indifferent to the charms of the new idol.

Zhirinovsky not only promised to provide cheap vodka, raise pensions and salaries, and lower taxes, he crossed the Russian nationalist idea with a repartitioning of the world and offered his voters the exclusive use of Finland, the Baltics, India, Turkey, and even Afghanistan (while divvying up Poland with the Germans). The ominous specter of war and fascism loomed on the horizon. Frightened, the democrats stampeded to organize a single front to combat this universal evil. But a year went by, the terrible specter settled into a warm nook in the State Duma, began to look more respectable, grew a paunch, and turned into a bogeyman that father-democrats used to scare their wayward children and foreign imperialists.

No sooner had we overcome our fright than the snow melted and the rivers flowed. The spring was a turbulent one. With the first signs of vernal madness the State Duma passed a resolution to release those who took part in the October putsch. No sooner said than done. A week later, the amnestied coup-plotters triumphantly came out of the gates of Lefortovo Prison to be met by crowds of admirers. While the public demanded explanations, presidential aides hid from reporters or, averting their eyes, lied into the microphones that everything had been done without their knowledge.

Didn't they know that the State Duma had the right only to amnesty convicted criminals? That only the president has the right to pardon persons before trial? And that a fair amount of time had gone by since the State Duma had passed the unlawful resolution, during which the public prosecutor's arbitrary authorization could have been overruled? It seemed that they didn't want to make these distinctions, perhaps because they were afraid that in the course of an

investigation something might come out that the public
was better off not knowing. Or perhaps they had decided
to balance Zhirinovsky's opposition with a counterweight,
that bunch of October putschists. Or perhaps both were
true.

No sooner had Russian citizens managed to put their
dropped jaws back in place when once again the alarm bells
went off. It was another coup attempt. A mysterious document called "Version Number One" appeared in *Obschaya
gazeta* (Common Newspaper), then several days later, it was
followed by "Version Number Two." Both "versions," which
were anonymous political memos about a supposed plot
underway to overthrow the president, named a number of
leading government figures who were encroaching on the
president's authority. Although both versions of the plot
turned out to be plants, the security services and the mass
media spent a whole month trying to track them down,
"pouring from the empty into the void," as we say in Russian. The scandal died down as quickly as it had erupted,
buried under a shroud of secrecy. But speculation continued.
Some said that the elite groups were trying to intimidate each
other. Others said that this was an attempt to rile the public
and provoke premature "actions." Level-headed *Izvestia*
summed it up best: "Things have become more and more
strange in Russia. The anonymous writers did not explode
the political situation as much as they lent clarity to the state
of insanity that has seized our society."[19]

The late President Richard Nixon, who visited Moscow in March 1994, made a clinical diagnosis: "Russia's political scene can only be described as chaotic."[20] Well, as we
say here, he wasn't discovering America, but he did pour
some oil on the fire of Russian passions, which already were

fiercely burning, by meeting with leaders of the Russian opposition. This put Yeltsin in an incredible rage. Meanwhile
the former American president was praising Grigory Yavlin-
sky, "an impressive young economist"; Sergei Shakhrai, then
minister of nationalities affairs, as "possessing an analytical
mind"; and Alexander Shokhin, "the brilliant minister of the
economy." All of them—Yeltsin's rivals—were "good potential presidential material." The axe still fell on their too-
clever heads several months later, hurting the careers of the
presidential hopefuls.

We got through the summer fairly peacefully, thank
God, digging in our gardens; they even managed to pass the
budget for 1994. (And yet why bother? After all, we'd lived
half a year without it!) We withdrew our forces from Germany and didn't even get into any fights. The general picture of well-being achieved by the Agreement on Civic
Accord (signed by the president and all the warring parliamentary factions) was spoiled a little by the specter of
war with Ukraine, which kept appearing and disappearing
into the fog. Russia simply could not find a way to share
with Ukraine either its nuclear warheads or Sevastopol and
the Black Sea Fleet. They both began tugging the Crimean
Peninsula back and forth, like poor divorced spouses who
are forced to sleep in the same bed, tugging on the same
blanket.

Of course there was the famous MMM scandal at
the end of the summer, but no one took it seriously
back then and people—except for the victimized MMM
"partners"—were genuinely having a good time. We even
began to put aside a little money. Life seemed to be settling
down a little bit and the light was visible at the end of the
tunnel.

Then came the end of our quiet life. Starting in the middle of October, it was off to hell in a handbasket. October 11 marked Black Tuesday, the day the ruble plunged in value more than 30 percent, provoking a total panic. Many people raced to buy dollars—and lost their shirts because the government issued a decree the next day restoring the previous exchange rate. Those who knew in advance bought rubles that day and made a killing for themselves—and there were quite a few in the know.

It was too bad that prices, which skyrocketed when the ruble collapsed, could not be restored, despite harsh measures by the city government. All sorts of versions of the story were floating around, and various parties were blamed—the Central Bank, Prime Minister Chernomyrdin in cahoots with the Ministry of Finance, the Judeo-Masonic conspirators, and some devious foreign capitalists. The president himself, who finally spoke up after a prolonged silence, even uttered the terrible word *sabotage* as an explanation for the crash and assigned people of military rank to investigate the matter, raising the old specter of the terror in the 1930s. The state security services quickly found a scapegoat—the commercial banks, against whom the central government financial agencies had long been sharpening their knives, claiming that the private banks were siphoning off depositors' capital. The world of finance seemed mired in the clutches of the security agencies.

At the end of October the agitated swamp of Russian life almost oozed over the edges after the murder of twenty-seven-year-old journalist Dmitry Kholodov, a reporter for the newspaper *Moskovskiy Komsomolets* who had covered war stories and was investigating corruption in the Russian Western Group of Forces.* His murder was so brazen and brutal that the world once again shuddered at Russian barbarism. And once again it was a mystery who had killed him and why. Kholodov's chief enemies continued to hang on to their comfortable seats, and the president, in a gesture of solidarity with Defense Minister Grachev who had been criticized by Kholodov, did not attend his funeral. This provoked a storm of outrage and cost him 60 percent of his approval ratings.

But that was not the main thing. After Kholodov's murder, threats began to be heard openly for the first time about the presence of some mysterious and brutal "third force" ruthlessly seeking power. The journalist Alexander Minkin hinted darkly in an interview that if the newspaper's exposure of corruption pointed to Defense Minister Grachev or other military officials and led to their downfall, worse people could come in their place: "Are we actually clearing the way for someone else? That would be terrible—imagine, you fire a thief, and you get a murderer! And that murderer will rub his hands and say, 'Thanks, guys!'"

Someone, invisible and ruthless, was destabilizing society. All these incidents seemed like links in the same chain—MMM, Black Tuesday, and the murder of Kholodov. All of it sent chills up and down one's spine.

Journalists had only just written the last sentence in their up-to-the-minute reports when the target moved again.

---

* Kholodov had investigated allegations of corruption within the Russian forces in Germany. He received an anonymous telephone tip advising him that confirmation of his story could be found in a briefcase in a locker. When he opened the attaché case in his office, it exploded, killing him and wounding a colleague. High-ranking military officials were alleged to have been involved in ordering his assassination.—TRANS.

This time it was the elections in Mytishchinsky District, when MMM president Mavrodi landed a seat in the State Duma. It made everyone feel even worse. "The dress rehearsal before the premiere," the journalists dubbed Mavrodi's election. When you took a look at the slate of candidates (a pyramid schemer, a fascist, a person close to the mafia, a party bureaucrat), then at the way the elections were conducted (blatant purchase of votes, intimidation, fraud, demagogic promises, ballot-box stuffing), and then finally at the social status and passivity of the voters (less than 25 percent turnout), it wasn't too hard to figure out how the next parliamentary and presidential elections would go, and whom our wise people would elect.

The events whirled together like slivers of glass in a kaleidoscope. Personnel shuffles in the highest echelons of power came thick and fast. Your eyes glazed over. Vice premiers and ministers, presidential staff workers spun like shadows in a magic lantern. Famous people and familiar faces disappeared from the scene and strangers took their place. Those who tried to follow what was happening finally threw up their hands in defeat. Only one thing was clear: there was a struggle for power going on behind the scenes.

December opened with another bloodbath. For some reason that has become quite the tradition with us—the most pleasant surprises are always sprung on us before New Year's (like the invasion of Afghanistan in December 1979). The conflict in Chechnya (with Russia's very active participation) was reaching a conclusive phase.* In the name of "defend-

---

* Russia considered Chechnya to be part of its territory despite Chechnya's declaration of independence in 1991.—TRANS.

ing" the constitution, unmarked planes began bombing
Grozny, the capital of Chechnya, and Russian soldiers and
officers, hired by the Federal Counterintelligence Service
(FSK) to sacrifice their lives for the ridiculous sum of $2,000,
attacked the presidential palace in tanks. Yeltsin announced
ominously that if the Chechens did not settle things themselves within forty-eight hours, Russia would declare a state
of emergency.

There were too few mercenaries (posing as soldiers
of the Chechen opposition) and the untrained infantry scattered, the offensive crumbled, some of the attackers were
killed, and some were taken hostage by the Chechens who
gleefully held up the "Russian aggressors" to the whole
world. Then the real Russian surrealism began, leaving many
people who watched on television speechless. For several days
everyone disowned the Russian hostages—the FSK and
Army General Grachev, who was suddenly suffering from
temporary amnesia. With a little smirk, Grachev claimed
that he couldn't know what was going on in each specific
division of the army. The hostages also lied, as if they didn't
know what they were getting into—supposedly they had
been promised a nice cakewalk through an unpopulated
Grozny to be followed by greetings with flowers. They also
said that they had been "set up" (never explaining by
whom)—that for some reason they had been forced to paint
their tanks white before the attack and after the operation
was over they were ordered to assemble at the Grozny air-
port where, as it later turned out, President Dudayev of
Chechnya had concentrated his strongest combat troops. Realizing that a decision had been made to get rid of them as
witnesses, or perhaps because they had simply chickened out
(after all, taking pot shots at the White House in Moscow

was a breeze, and could even get you a star on your epaulets), these poor excuses for mercenaries preferred to give themselves up to the enemy.

Meanwhile, a few days later, the heads of the Russian security ministries suddenly got over their amnesia, by which time the tragedy with the hostages had turned into a farce. Members of parliament flocked to Chechnya trying to win points before the presidential race. Dudayev personally gave each of them a few of the Russian lads as a Christmas present.

General Grachev held talks with Dudayev, Yeltsin seemed to forget about his threat to declare a state of emergency, armored vehicles massed on the Chechnya border, security was reinforced in Moscow at certain strategic buildings because of the threat of Chechen terrorists, and in Chechnya itself on the main square of the capital, militant mountaineers performed war dances and formed detachments of suicide fighters. Russia was slowly but surely being drawn into the quagmire of a war reminiscent of Afghanistan.

There was so much furor around this development that it completely deafened another scandal that same week in Moscow. On December 2, armed to the teeth (even with army grenade launchers), unidentified persons in frightful black masks blocked the building of the mayor's office throughout the day. This building is also the location of the Most financial group's offices (one of the groups blamed for Black Tuesday). The unknown assailants beat the guards of Most banker Vladimir Gusinsky and when the police, and then the Moscow counterintelligence service, arrived on the scene, the masked men refused to answer questions. After a violent clash, the two sides finally went their separate ways in peace. The public was kept in suspense for several days, and finally, three days later, the Presidential Security Service—essentially Yeltsin's palace guard—and Russia's Chief Directorate of Security "took responsibility" for the incident.

Their press service distributed a statement that they "had conducted an investigation of a tip concerning the fact of the presence of unidentified armed persons in a motorcade in an area that is part of the zone of responsibility of federal agencies of state security." This was a deliberate lie. General Savostyanov, who had given the order to seize the unidentified special-assignment troops in masks (something quite logical under the conditions of growing terrorism), paid for his boldness in interfering in the affairs of the presidential security agencies by being fired from his job as head of Moscow's counterintelligence.

I remember my shock as I followed the television coverage of armed men who looked like murderers in the very center of Moscow, to the utter bewilderment of passersby—the impression was more vivid than watching a gangster movie. Political commentator Yevgeny Kiselev, anchor for the Sunday television news analysis program *Itogi* (Summation), ended his show that day with old newsreels of the murder of Sergei Kirov, which sparked the Stalinist era of terror. With a surprising note of hysteria in his voice, Kiselev expressed the wish that the show's producers would not be gagged and that "we will meet again on the air next Sunday."

Stunned, I turned off the television and sat for two hours staring blankly at the wall, my only thought, "Lord, just what is going on here?!" Then my reasoning faculties returned to me and I began to fantasize—what would happen to us if . . .

∾

In the Russian emigre author Vladimir Voinovich's novel *Moscow 2042*, one of the heroes—an "authoritarian giant"—is a writer named Karnavalov who says, "Your much-vaunted democracy doesn't suit us Russians. A situation where every fool can express his opinion and tell the authorities what they should or shouldn't do is not for us. We need a single ruler who wields absolute authority and knows exactly where to go and why."[21]

Voinovich writes this satirically; in fact, this comment reveals a very unpalatable but interesting idea. In Russia these days, no matter where you spit you'll hit a politician. But most Russian politicians are as ephemeral as apple blossoms floating on the river. The wind blows—and where have they gone? They are no more. But Russia is used to Rulers. That's how it has been raised. In order to become a real Ruler, it's not enough to be a politician. It's not enough to head up a faction or even a party. In Russia, to be a Ruler you have to be a person of the System. The System, a living octopus-like organism, is always more important than mere politicians. The System is imperishable and irreplaceable. The octopus whips its tentacle—and a politician is gone. How many episodes like that have occurred in Russian history! Only a few individuals have been able to get the better of the System.

So what about those talented forty-year-old boys that Nixon so highly admired? It's only too clear now that they won't become the chosen ones, in the near future at any rate. We don't have to look far to find examples of this—let us recall the elections in Mytishchinsky District and December

12, 1993, when the darkest of dark horses came first to the finish line. In a country where the people are accustomed to Rulers and the System, where the mass mind is at the level of feudal society, where the elect are driven by cynicism and selfishness, universal suffrage can be as dangerous as a revolution or a nuclear bomb.

Valeriya Novodvorskaya, a well-known opposition figure, wrote in a witty article, "The Russian Mafia-state's Mytishchi-gate":

> The democratic opposition will proclaim the ideas of Westernizing the primal hordes and rogues like Mavrodi and Co., appearing on the same platform as the red-browns, and will simply buy out the electoral commissions lock, stock, and barrel. That is, some will come to kill, others to buy, and still others to preach eternal truths to pogromists, idiots, and swindlers. Those aren't elections, but a madhouse. They should be postponed for about ten years. Universal suffrage is like a suit we buy to grow into. Let it hang in the closet for a while. Eyeglasses, of course, are a sign of civilization, but can you consider civilized that monkey from the fable who didn't know how to wear glasses and put them on his tail?[22]

After television commentator Kiselev's memorable farewell to his audience, I could not get to sleep for a long time. I kept trying to imagine what would happen if say, well, not even a junta, but some abstract oligarchic clique came to power. I realized that nothing fundamentally new would happen to us.

There would likely not be any more bloodshed, nor social rebellions and revolutions. The authorities won't allow it. Besides, there wouldn't be anybody to revolt—people got their fill of that in 1991 and 1993. Furthermore, those who come to power will take a harder line than the fools who packed Moscow with armored vehicles in 1991 but failed to take power. The new ones won't even have to shoot anyone—they'll just jump out of their cars in black masks with grenade launchers and throw everyone face down in the snow with their hands behind their backs. They have been well trained to take over without a single gunshot. They won't touch the post of the president—why bother? It will only frighten the international community with our usual outrageousness. Oligarchic cliques can quite easily coexist with presidents, even preserving the romantic image of democratic rule. The only problem is, who will be president?

The elections, of course, will be postponed and the parliament dispersed so those chattering and confusing people don't interfere with building the "new life." Parties will be banned and a state of emergency and a curfew will most likely be imposed—to the sheer delight of ordinary folk. Street crime will drop drastically.

Rich competitors will not have to be hung from the lamp posts as in October 1917. Those who cooperate with the System will get their share, and the rivals will be plucked off, unless they manage to flee to their villas and apartments in Paris, Miami, or Nice. Small and medium vendors and entrepreneurs will not be touched and will even be supported: they make up half the country now anyway and the new authorities will have to rely on someone! The tradespeople will support strong rule; it will be a good government for them. And if some social benefits and aid to the needy are tossed out, the people will follow such a government even to the execution block!

On the other hand the intelligentsia, especially the press, will be gagged and censorship, or self-censorship, imposed. The borders will be sealed again. Of course there will be the secret police—people in our country aren't reasonable, especially the creative types, and need constant watching. Ordinary people will be indifferent, as long as they have love stories and hockey games on the television, and cheap sausage and vodka—they don't need freedom of speech.

Very soon we will all march in neat rows and columns, singing songs about building a "free market" and a new economy, naively listening to news roundups of imperialist plots and the increase in milk production in Saratov district. Because democracy is not suitable for our people who, as Voinovich wrote, always promote from among their ranks one who knows "exactly where he is going." What sort of government system will this be? The latest model corrective labor colony of the strictest regimen. No wonder they've always written about American prisons in our country with such admiration. Who's to blame? We ourselves are to blame.

Most interestingly, the world community will not be very indignant about such a government in Russia because they are fed up with Russian anarchy and terribly afraid of the Russian-Caucasian mafia and the poorly guarded nuclear facilities. Everything else is Russia's own internal affair, especially if the new regime announces that reforms will continue full speed ahead, if on a special, Russian path.

Will I feel sorry for Russian democracy? I have to

say no. How can you feel sorry for something that never even existed?

Will I feel sorry for the lost faith in the radiant future? Again, no. Because I never harbored any particular illusions regarding Russian reform, although I did have some hopes for the reasonableness of both the people and the rulers, which is why I voted for reform and for the constitution during the referendum.

Will I feel sorry for the lost freedom? Freedom of speech, freedom of spirit, freedom of conscience, freedom of movement and choice, and, finally, the loss of glasnost? Yes, I will be unbearably sorry! Because that is the only thing that we wrested for ourselves from the System in the last few nightmarish years, our chief, remarkable victory. If they take that away, what will be left in life?

A country that doesn't laugh is a sick country. People who have lost their sense of humor are unwell. You can expect unpleasant surprises from them.

We had many surprises during this astonishing year, but shortly before the New Year, we got the greatest of them all—civil war. The mad military machine lurched into motion, grinding up in its inexorable steel maw both innocent and guilty, babies and professional killers, inexperienced boy soldiers and criminally inept generals. All of Russia writhed in an unbearable torment of empathy, despair, and pain.

New Year's Eve stands out in particular in this endless nightmare. It was the apotheosis of the year. While we in Moscow sat in front of our glowing television screens next to our twinkling Christmas trees, there was a war in the capital of Chechnya and people were dying. Death-dealing shells exploded, Russian tanks burned like holiday wreaths, and teenagers trapped inside their molten bellies were incinerated, dispatched to a senseless and unnecessary death. For many civilians, the first day of the New Year was their last. The dawning of the gloomy morning laid bare a terrible scene: burned-out armored vehicles with drivers turned to charcoal, piles of corpses on the streets, devastated residential buildings lying in ruins. Corpses lay on the scorched earth, picked at by dogs and cats frenzied by the scent of blood, as snipers' bullets whistled overhead.

Through a wall left gaping by a shell, the television camera panned over the defiled interior of an empty apartment. A modest New Year's repast was still on the table; silver tinsel from a little artificial tree waved in the freezing wind. The residents, who only a few hours ago had been sitting at this table and admiring the tree, were no longer there, although it seemed their voices continued to echo and their shadows flickered across the walls. Had they managed to get out or had they died? How unbearably hard it must have been to die on New Year's Eve!

The holiday felt strange in Moscow as well, with the pouring rain, no smiles or toasts, and surrounded by the terrible specters of civil war and revolution, a great Caucasian war and battle with the Islamic world, bloody chaos, dictatorship, and impending destruction. Suddenly we were gazing into a horrible bottomless pit and sensing that something unspeakably ghastly had brushed against us.

Only on January 7, Russian Orthodox Christmas, did the snow begin to fall, virginally pure and innocent, blanketing this whole nightmare like a shroud, like a sign, a symbol that God had heard the cries of the innocent and would not allow a repeat of this hell, and that time would knit and heal—someday, perhaps—the terrible wounds rending the earth and people's souls. This snow of the purest white covered up the nastiness of Moscow, the slush and the lies, just as it covered the charred Chechen land and the dead bodies in puddles of blood, and appeared to freeze for a moment the heat of fury, the thirst for revenge, and the insanity. It seemed to be calling on everyone to come to their senses and stop. It was the phantom snow of our timid and phantom hope.

Epilogue

Coming Together

There is a clever children's game, a cross between a mosaic and a brainteaser that requires the reassembly of a scrambled puzzle of different-colored cardboard pieces within a frame. It takes hellish patience and a keen eye to take the formless pile of eyes, ears, noses, feet, pieces of swords, clothes, horses' hooves, and dogs' tails, and find the first two pieces that fit exactly together. Then you have to sort through the pile, trying different pieces and setting them aside, and then rooting again through the colorful heap until you can put the picture together.

I have spent almost a year putting together a puzzle like this: searching, watching, listening closely, trying to fathom, asking questions, digging; sorting pieces and fragments, and sticking them together. Sometimes the pieces didn't fit, the picture fell apart, and I had to mix them up and start over again. Finally the disconnected fragments came together, obeying the hidden logic of the whole. What has emerged is what you see: a picture in a frame. It is made up of pieces—here is crime, there is irresponsibility; here is politics, but there is the everyday life of ordinary people dependent on politics; here is the mafia, and there is the corrupted government; here is personal dignity and humiliation, there is slumbering national pride. I have written about medical care, culture, art, religion, sects, psychology, television, and education—the background of our inner life. I have covered the economy as well as everyday life and the stores, which are its concrete manifestation.

The whole world knows that Russia is conducting some grandiose reforms, although nobody really seems to understand what they're all about. The whole world has heard that Russia is building democracy, although no one has any idea how it will turn out. No one can explain why the living standard is falling in Russia, why industry is slowing down and collapsing, why people don't feel like working. How can these things be if there is reform and democracy?!

In the picture I have assembled from the myriad fragments, you will find answers to some of these questions. You saw some of the main characters in our drama—the rich and the poor, the intelligentsia and the outcasts, the old and the young, the workers and the new Russians, the rulers and the common folk. Everyone can find something of interest in this mosaic.

Some readers will probably say that Russia isn't like this. "I've been to Moscow myself," they'll say. "I've traveled around Russia and even lived there, and I didn't see anything like this." That's true. You wouldn't see things like this out of the window of a five-star hotel or fancy tourist bus, much less from a government limousine. It's a different angle. You can probably live more affluently and have a far better time in Moscow on a salary of $3,000 a month than you can in

New York. However, this does not deny the existence of my world—it is quite real, although very depressing. After all, from the very beginning of this book, I promised to show you a Russia that isn't laughing.

I can imagine the criticism from the other extreme, people accusing me of contempt for the Motherland, of mud-slinging. We Russians have lied to ourselves for so long, to the people and to the whole world, that we have managed to merge completely with our own deception. We have grown used to being great and mighty, unequaled in the world. We have become accustomed to covering our bodies with an intricate lace of propaganda, not realizing that the skin underneath is scabbed and our insides completely infected. We have grown used to our own flattery, our own eulogizing, and now, when we hear the unpleasant truth—from outsiders or our own—we fall into a sanctimonious rage, whether we are rulers or commoners. It is very hard to reconcile yourself to the fact that you are no longer great and mighty, but rather third-rate, something hideous and pathetic.

Of course I could have told some white lies. That would not be lying so much as softening, touching up, applying some rouge, and blowing rainbow-colored bubbles. I could hold up a clear, impenetrable mirror to the reader who is curious by nature, and he would see a clear sky, white clouds, and colorfully dressed peasants dancing in a circle on a mowed field. But something makes you want to look closer—to the other side of the looking glass, beyond the famous Russian reforms. Then we see behind the mirror, just as in the home of a shiftless housewife, a lot of dust and filth, dead flies, hole-filled socks, and all sorts of long-forgotten things.

But let us not fall into hopeless pessimism. Let us

recall that this world is only one of Russia's many parallel worlds, and not all of its inhabitants are thieves, murderers, swindlers, and freeloaders. Of course there are law-abiding, hard-working people, too, although they find it very difficult now. There is hope. It's just that we cannot lie, at least not to ourselves, and we must make a precise diagnosis of the illness. Only then is healing possible.

On the whole, the reserve of strength of spirit and endurance in Russia surely amazes everyone. I personally do not know of a single other country in the world that has been so trampled, tormented, and tortured for so many centuries, but where the people have still preserved their humanity. Even now in our time of troubles, when the whole country is like a rudderless ship dashing through the waves, or like a madhouse where even the doctors have lost their minds, ordinary human life goes on in Russia—which is simply incomprehensible. Just as in the prosperous countries, ordinary human activity continues: people fall in love, marry, and have children. Just as in the old days, ballerinas light as swan feathers flit across the stage, athletes break world records, and cosmonauts circle the earth in spaceships. Sadly, however, there is less and less of this, and ordinary human happiness is harder and harder to come by.

Still, I want to believe in the dream of a new life because we now have something we never had before: openness and glasnost. Though incomplete, it is still freedom. There is finally a crack in the fear—the ancient slavish fear before the masters.

Indeed, if we Russians have not attained democracy in the last few years, we have, nonetheless, acquired priceless, although bitter experience: we now know exactly how democracy is *not* supposed to be. Knowing that, it will be easier to separate the wheat from the chaff.

Some Russians have already been corrupted and have irreversibly turned into freeloaders and spongers. That is lamentable, but the job now is to reach out to those who want to work, want to earn an honest living, to those with skillful hands and bright minds. Russia has always been rich in talent. But the talent, like gold nuggets, is very scattered, trampled in the mud, or hidden under a bushel. Thus we Russians, known for our alienation from each other, must learn to come together.

Before the first ray of light shines, possibly more than one generation must pass. Time must sweep from the stage not only the old Communist mastodons but the younger, more agile, cynical bureaucrats, today's "democrats," who are just as heavily corrupted by the lie. Then the real new generation will come, people who truly know the worth of hard work and money. These men and women are in their twenties now, or even younger. They have a strong immunity to any kind of politics and ideology. How wonderful it is that our young people are so apolitical! Less politics means less filth, less scrambling for a position, and more real work, and, it would seem, more prosperity for the country. My main hope is in these young people.

Recently we celebrated my daughter's tenth birthday. She invited thirteen children, almost half of her classmates. I really liked these kids—they were clear-eyed, lively, quick, and very knowledgeable. They could think for themselves, were not bound by stereotypes, and knew how to behave and have a good time. They were worlds apart from the ten-year-old Pioneer children of my youth. My daughter's friends were *very* grownup, with very grownup thoughts. They will mature into individuals who know what they want and how to get it. True, they were all children of rich or very well-to-do parents, but even so—and this surprised me most of all—they had none of that nouveau riche arrogance or snobbery, or that upper-class attitude of "anything goes."

No one bragged about his or her parents' wealth or the number of computers or television sets in their home—those things were seen as something quite ordinary. For these children there was something more important: who could dance, or sing, or recite poetry the best; who knew the Bible better or had read the most books. In short—who was winning. These kids were articulate and had something to show for themselves. It was obvious that in their adult lives they would play and win just as persistently and purposefully.

I watched the children closely because I suddenly realized what has to be done in order to drag our country out of the quagmire. We have to realize our responsibility to this young generation. We have to create such favorable conditions for *all* children, even at the price of some great sacrifices. We have to make the starting line equal for all of them, so none will be deprived, humiliated, rejected, angered, or impoverished; so that there will be no reason for envy and revenge; so that they will not have to steal, sell their bodies, or dream of going abroad. We have to ensure that the values of these little people are measured not by the number of tape decks in their homes or sticks of smoked sausage in their refrigerators but by knowledge and the ability to do something well and earn honest money—so that all the children in our country will be as clear-eyed and as confident of themselves and their future as those who came to my daughter's birthday party.

Now *that* would mean the first green shoots of real democracy. Is it utopian? Perhaps. My Lord, how much time, patience, and effort—and money, of course—will be required for this? But the main thing, first, is to wish for it with all our hearts.

Notes

1. O. Latsis, "Na puti k stabilizatsi nakhodilas ekonomika Rossii pri peretry-aske pravitelstva" [Russian Economy on Road to Stabilization with Government Shake-Up], *Izvestia*, January 29, 1994.
2. "Padeniye urovnya zhizni: mif ili realnost" [Fall in Living Standard: Myth or Reality?], *Izvestia*, February 17, 1994.
3. O. Latsis, "Ekonomika Rossii Na Dne. Ne pora li podnimatsya?" [Russian Economy Hits Bottom: Time to Rise?], *Izvestia*, January 28, 1994.
4. S. Govorukhin, *Velikaya kriminalnaya revolyutsia* [*The Great Criminal Revolution*] (Moscow: Andreevsky flag, 1993), pp. 34, 35–36, 38–39, 41.
5. "U Mafii svoi vzglyady na predstoyashchiye vybory . . . i plany tozhe" [The Mafia Has Its Own Views of Upcoming Elections . . . and Plans, Too], *Argumenty i fakty*, no. 39 (October 1992).
6. Lewis Carroll, *Through the Looking Glass and What Alice Found There* (New York: William Morrow, 1993), 40–41.
7. Stanislav Govorukhin, "Strana vorov na doroge v svetloe budschee," *Kuranty*, May 5, 1992, p. 5.
8. L. N. Tolstoy, *Anna Karenina*, trans. Rosemary Edmonds (New York: Penguin Books, 1977), p. 13.

9. V. Pankov, "My nikogda ne stavili zadachu sdelat kazhdogo grazhdanina sobstvennikom" [We Never Set the Goal of Making Every Citizen a Property Owner], *Financial Times*, March 24–30, 1994.

10. "Pisma v MMM" [Letters to MMM], *Izvestiya*, August 10, 1994.

11. S. Buntman, daily morning political commentary on Echo Moscow radio station, November 1, 1994.

12. I. Milshtein, "V razvode" [Divorced], in the Position section, *Ogonyok* (March 1993), p. 8.

13. A. Terekhov, "Tsvet zavtrashnego dnya" [Color of Tomorrow], *Ogonyok* (March 1991), p. 1.

14. *Iks press: Gazeta chastnogo intimnogo pisma* [X Press: Newspaper of Private Intimate Letters] (August 1993), p. 8.

15. *Iks press: Gazeta chastnogo intimnogo pisma* [X Press: Newspaper of Private Intimate Letters] (August 1993), p. 34.

16. Shusaku Endo, *Silence*, trans. William Johnston (New York: Taplinger, 1980), 240.

17. O. Latsis, "Poddelnaya Rossiya ne pomozhet dukhovnomu vozrozhdeniyu obshchestva" [A False Russia Will Not Help the Spiritual Renewal of Society], *Izvestia*, November 24, 1994.

18. A. Vinogradov, "V ozhidanii spasitelya" [In Expectation of a Savior], *Segodnya*, no. 57 (1995).

19. V. Ivanizdze, "Uzhe 'versiya no. 2' gosperevorota s faishivym faksom otpravitelya gulyayet po vazhnym kabinetam" [Now "Version no. 2" of a Coup d'Etat with a False Fax from the Sender is Spreading Through Important Offices], *Izvestia*, March 25, 1994.

20. Richard Nixon, "Na rossiyskoy politicheskoy stsene tsarit khaos" [Russia's Political Scene Can Only Be Described as Chaotic], *Izvestia*, March 31, 1994.

21. Vladimir Voinovich, *Moscow 2042*, trans. Richard Lourie (New York: Harcourt Brace Jovanovich, 1987), 74.

22. V. Novodvorskaya, "Mytishchigeyt rossiyskoy okhlokratii" [The Russian Mafia-state's Mytishchi-gate], *Novy vzglyad*, no. 143 (1994).

Index

adolescents, *see* children and adolescents
Afghanistan, 213, 215
Agreement on Civic Accord, 210
ambulances, 37, 66, 68–69
Andropov, Yuri, xiii, 130
Animal Farm (Orwell), 75
Anna Karenina (Tolstoy), 85
Arbat (shopping mall), 99, 106
Armenians, xiii, 13, 23, 65
arts, *see* culture and art
Asahara, Shoko, 198, 199
astrology, 203
Aum Shinrikyo, 198, 199, 206
Azerbaijanis, 13, 23

banks, 33
    Central Bank, 153, 157, 211
    cheating by, 32
    mafia and, 45
    wages in, 30
barbiturates, 109
Berdyayev, Nikolai, 128, 129
black market, 31, 89, 107, 156
Black Tuesday, 160, 211, 215
blat (connections), 47–48, *see also* mafia
Blok, Alexander, 183
bombs, 35, 37, 41, 43
books, 14, 82, 175–176
Borovoy, Konstantin, 160
Brezhnev, Leonid, xiii, 13, 92, 144, 183, 196
bribery, 6, 7, 23, 112, 142
Buntman, Sergei, 161

cars
    availability of, 139

credit purchase of, 151
    hitchhiking and, 40
    theft of, 38, 39
Catherine II, 196
censorship, 220
Central Bank, 153, 157, 211
Chechnya, 213–215, 221–223
Chernenko, Konstantin, xiii
children and adolescents, 94–101, 102–112, 229–230
    abandoned, 99, 126
    culture and, 97–98, 102–103
    and discos, 111
    drug use by, 109–110
    education of, 22, 23, 96–99, 107–108, 110, 112
    homeless, 101
    and juvenile crime, 99–101, 105, 107
    kidnapping of, 36–37, 125
    mortality rate, 83–84
    music and, 103, 106, 109
    of new Russians, 87–90, 96–98, 104–105
    physical ailments of, 53–54, 66, 68–71
    politics and, 112, 123–124
    of poor families, 98–101
    of prosperous families, 96–98
    as prostitutes, 99, 100, 185–186
    safety of, 34, 36–37, 110, 176
    totalitarian sects and, 201–202, 203
Christianity, 116, 192–197
Chubais, Anatoly, 130–133
Church of Christ, 198
civil war, 221–223
cocaine, 109

About the Author

Galina Borisovna Dutkina was born in 1952 in the small city of Tambov in central Russia, and grew up in Moscow. She graduated from the Institute of Asian and African Studies at Moscow State University with a major in History and Oriental Studies, and earned a doctorate in Philology. She has worked as an editor and announcer at Moscow Radio, and as an editor at the publishing house Raduga Press. Dutkina has translated many works of literature and nonfiction from the English and Japanese languages into Russian. She is a member of the Russian Union of Journalists and the Union of Translators, and is currently working in Moscow as a journalist and lecturer on Japanese culture and literature.